BUSES
YEARBOOK 1999

Edited by
STEWART J. BROWN

IAN ALLAN
Publishing

First published 1998

ISBN 0 7110 2594 0

Published by Ian Allan Publishing

an imprint of Ian Allan Publishing Ltd,
Terminal House, Station Approach,
Shepperton, Surrey TW17 8AS.
Printed by Ian Allan Printing Ltd
Riverdene Business Park, Molesey
Road, Hersham, Surrey KT12 4RG

Code: 9808/F2

Front cover:
This was once Midland Red! Midlands it may
be, red it ain't . . . a 1998 Plaxton (formerly
Northern Counties)-bodied Scania L113, 1422
(R422 TJW) of Arriva Midlands North in
Tamworth. The Scania was one of
comparatively few non-low-floor single-deckers
delivered in 1998. Chris Morrison

Back cover, upper:
London Transport route 19 was the first won
under the tendering system by a non-London
buses company. LT supplied the Routemasters,
under contract, to Kentish Bus, which painted
them in this attractive livery. Now, in Arriva
ownership, they are back in LT-style red under
the auspices of Arriva London South.

Back cover, lower:
Most of Stagecoach's Interurban coaches are
Volvo 12m B10Ms. However, one of the first
batches was built on 11m Dennis Javelin, 27
of which are with Ribble. 164 (L106 SDY), on
the long-established X43 Manchester-Burnley
service (it used to run through to Skipton) is
one of seven soon transferred from
Stagecoach South, and is seen at Burnley. It is
unusual for a Plaxton Premiere in having
opening windows.

Title page:
Part of the busy central bus station in
Bangalore with local buses and milling
passengers.
Alistair Douglas

Contents

The Thistle
COMES FULL CIRCLE

Gavin Booth

The Scottish press tends to describe FirstBus as 'Aberdeen-headquartered', acknowledging that it is not really a Scottish company in the way that Stagecoach can claim to be, but at least it has its operational head office in Aberdeen. The fact is that an important element of FirstBus is decidedly Scottish, with roots in the Grampian Bus Group and, a century ago, in Aberdeen Corporation's transport department.

Looking back, Grampian was an unlikely basis for the group that now runs Britain's biggest bus fleet. Aberdeen Corporation had been a medium-size municipal fleet with 230-odd buses in 1975 when Grampian Regional Transport took over. GRT became a limited company in 1986 in the lead-up to deregulation and the creation of arm's-length municipal companies, and celebrated its new freedom by

competing with Scottish Bus Group's Northern Scottish company, also Aberdeen-based, but serving a large part of Scotland's northeast corner. As in Scotland's other cities, the former municipal operator spread beyond its traditional boundaries and the local SBG company started urban routes.

Below:
GRT bought an articulated Mercedes-Benz O.405G which is based in Aberdeen but has been tried by other group companies. It has a 60-seat three-door Alexander body. FirstGroup is buying articulated buses — Wright-bodied Volvos — in 1998.
ALL PHOTOGRAPHS BY THE AUTHOR

The first hint of GRT's wider ambitions came in 1987 when it bought the local coach and minibus operator, Mair of Bucksburn, which continued as a separate entity. GRT's ambitions were consolidated when it negotiated a management/employee buyout in 1988 — the first in Scotland and one of the first in the UK. GRT was fortunate that the company was not offered on the open market, as it would surely have proved to be an attractive buy for one of the emerging groups. A new company, GRT Holdings, took over in January 1989.

In its first year, GRT Holdings' acquisitions were local and low-key: coach operator Kirkpatrick of Banchory, and the routes of the failed Alexander (North East) company. But the privatisation of the Scottish Bus Group saw GRT move up a notch. It bid for the Lowland company, the first SBG company to be put on the market, but — as, strangely, often seems to be the case — this went to its management and employees. Undeterred it bid for others, winning Midland Scottish in 1990. With some 280 buses based in central Scotland, this greatly increased GRT's influence and before long Midland's blue/cream livery was being applied in GRT style, and GRT's trademark thistle dotting the 'i' in its fleetnames was applied to the word 'Bluebird' — but not the word 'Midland'.

The sale of Northern Scottish to Stagecoach in 1991 brought these two growing groups into contact, but a sensible rationalisation of routes in and around Aberdeen prevented any wasteful head-to-head competition, and the two companies appeared to live fairly happily together.

The Grampian fleet inherited in 1989 was typical of a medium-sized municipal operator with around 200 buses. Roundly nine out of every 10 buses were double-deckers, with a few coaches, two MetroRiders, two Leopard/Alexander Y-types and seven Leyland Nationals to make

up the number. The double-deckers were all Alexander-bodied Leylands — over 150 Atlanteans and 30 Olympians. By 1997 the shape of the fleet had changed dramatically, with double-deckers representing barely half the fleet, replaced by significant deliveries of Mercedes-Benz O.405 single-deckers, including one articulated bus.

This carries an Alexander body, as do deliveries of Dennis Dart midibuses and Mercedes-Benz 709D minibuses, but the other full-size single-deckers have Wright and Optare bodies.

Midland's fleet was a typical SBG mix of standard types and more individual purchases. So there were over 70 Leyland Leopards with Alexander Y-type bodies, for many the archetypal SBG bus, plus smaller batches of Leopards with Alexander's dual-purpose T-type body, or Duple Dominant bodies. There were 25 Leyland Nationals, a number of Leyland Tigers with dual-purpose and coach bodies, and some 30 Seddon Pennine VIIs, inherited from Eastern Scottish following boundary changes in 1985. The double-deck fleet was dominated by 40 MCW Metrobuses with lowheight Alexander bodies, and smaller batches of Fleetlines and Ailsas.

A controlling interest in Midland's isolated Oban operation was sold in 1992 to Derek Stuart, formerly a senior SBG manager, and a new company, Oban & District, was formed. The buses wore a variation of Midland cream/blue livery.

The Midland acquisition was an early indication of GRT's wider ambitions, but it would be 1993 before the empire expanded beyond Scotland. In the rush to sell off municipal companies in that year, GRT picked up the Leicester and Northampton undertakings. Another indication was the creation of the GRT Bus Group as a prelude to stock market flotation in 1994. The same year three more recently privatised companies joined the group.

First, Eastern Counties was bought from its

management in July, and GRT inherited a fairly elderly fleet of 375 buses. Three months later there was more activity in Scotland. Midland's eastern neighbour, Eastern Scottish (trading as SMT) was bought from its management and employees, and a month later Eastern's eastern neighbour, Lowland Omnibuses, followed suit. SMT brought 370 buses and Lowland 160, adding substantially to the group's size.

The SMT fleet, like other former SBG fleets, had been starved of new buses in the countdown to privatisation, and bus replacement had been difficult for the management/ employee team. Like many companies, SMT had bought minibuses in the post-deregulation years, and had 100 Renaults, including 30 longer S75s bought after privatisation. Single-deck buses were mainly Seddon Pennine VIIs, 60 of them with Alexander Y-type or T-type bodies, though since privatisation 13 Volvo B10Bs had been acquired, along with Optare MetroRiders. There were Dennis Javelin and Leyland Tiger coaches, and a mixed bag of double-deckers: over 50 Ailsas, 29 Fleetlines, 41 Olympians, nine Volvo Citybuses, and 13 rare Leyland Lions.

Lowland's bus fleet was broadly similar, reflecting the company's previous existence as the Borders area of Eastern Scottish. So there were around 50 Seddon Pennine VIIs, seven Leyland Nationals, a mixed bag of Tigers (including four Ulsterbus-style Alexander Q-types with Volvo engines), eight Optare MetroRiders, seven Renault S56s, and a mixture of coaches — an AEC, several Bedfords, DAFs and Dennises, and a Fiat minicoach — mostly from local operators which had been acquired. There were five new Scania K113 coaches, and the vehicles for the unusual Border Courier services which carried passengers to the more remote parts of the area, and provided a service linking hospitals and health centres for samples and equipment, which were carried in a special rear compartment; the current Couriers were five Bedford VASs and a Leyland Swift, all with Reeve Burgess bodies.

Lowland had a small double-deck fleet — three Fleetlines, three secondhand Bristol VRTs, six Olympians

and a former demonstration Leyland Titan TN15.

In 1985, when SBG restructured to prepare for deregulation, the Eastern Scottish operating area had been drastically cut. It had lost its Glasgow area operations to Midland, along with its Linlithgow depot, and the Border and East Lothian operations went to the newly formed Lowland company. Now the two companies were together again under another group, and as time progressed the boundaries between Eastern and Lowland became less obvious.

One of the consequences of the larger group was the ability to move buses around between companies. It started with Grampian's Atlanteans; which appeared in the Midland, Eastern and Lowland fleets, and with a number of the newer Atlanteans still in service in Aberdeen, this cascading looks set to continue. For SBG companies with no history of Atlanteans, these were unusual fleet additions, but they quickly proved to be useful buses, often replacing SBG-issue Fleetlines. Midland Leopards found their way into the Leicester and Northampton fleets, and ex-Midland Metrobuses joined similar buses in Leicester. Leicester Metrobuses also found their way to Northampton, and an odd batch of Northampton Olympians with East Lancs bodies moved quickly to Grampian, which fairly soon moved them on to Eastern.

More significant was the spread of the GRT-style livery, though using local colours. So Midland buses had become cream/blue with GRT-style fleetnames, SMT buses were identical to Grampian's in cream/green, Leicester and Northampton adopted cream with two shades of red, and Eastern Counties became cream with red/orange. Lowland, another 'green' company, went for two shades of green on a yellow background to distinguish its buses from SMT's.

The GRT thistle motif appeared on fleetnames where this was possible — and even where it was not possible. On the Leicester Citybus fleet the thistle appeared above both 'i's; Northampton used it above the 'p'; Eastern Counties above the 'i'. Lowland stuck to its existing fleetname style, while SMT introduced two fleetnames — SMT Edinburgh and SMT Lothians — which, some cynics suggested, was simply to give the company an 'i' for the thistle. Although the idea was to separate out depot and service responsibilities, it meant little to passengers, particularly when Lowland buses operating in East Lothian were turned out in the same colours but with Lowland fleetnames.

With its growing empire, GRT had to start investing in new vehicles to replace ageing buses, particularly in the bus-starved former SBG fleets. From an early stage GRT adopted a quality approach, and it looked very much as if double-deckers were a thing of the past.

For the Aberdeen-based Grampian fleet there were new Mercedes-Benz O.405s, including the unique Alexander-bodied artic, registered K1 GRT, which visited other group companies in its first years in service. This had air-conditioning and double-glazing, and it seemed that this might become GRT standard. New rigid O.405s for Grampian had these features, as did Wright-bodied Scania N113 buses for Midland, but deliveries to other group companies had more typical specifications.

Grampian's original body order for its 1992/3 Mercedes-Benz was with Alexander, but in the event only the artic was built at Falkirk and the rigid Mercs were bodied at Ballymena by Wright. Subsequent O.405 deliveries in 1995-7 have carried Optare Prisma bodies. Alexander has

Above:
Among the more unusual vehicles operated by Lowland are four Leyland Tigers built to an Ulsterbus specification with Volvo engines and Alexander (Belfast) Q-type bodies. This is Lowland's version of the standard GRT livery.

Below:
In an earlier Lowland livery, the sole demonstration Leyland Titan heads towards central Edinburgh. It was acquired by Lowland with the business of Glass of Haddington and for some time was the only Titan in Scotland.

The Mercedes-Benz O.405/Optare Prisma combination was also built for Leicester in 1995, while Northampton received three Volvo B10Ls with Alexander Ultra bodies the same year.

SMT got 10 O.405/Prismas in 1995, and two Scania N113/Wright's for Midland were diverted to Lowland the same year. All of this was but a prelude to the changes that were to come. GRT had built up a reputation as an ambitious organisation with a good sense of quality and the importance of marketing, but it was still relatively small (just over 1,500 buses). The bus ownership trend in Britain was towards big groups like Stagecoach and British Bus, and, if it was to grow, GRT would need to find a willing partner.

The Badgerline Group had its roots in the country area of Bristol Omnibus, set up as a separate company in 1986 and privatised the same year, one of the first in the NBC sell-off. Like GRT it set about expanding by acquisition and grew substantially, mainly with former NBC companies, and with the purchase of the Rider Group, the former West Yorkshire PTE operation. It had size and influence, but was thought to lack GRT's flair. On their own, the two groups could have been prey to one of the larger groups; together they would be impregnable. So FirstBus was born in 1995, with 5,600 vehicles and operations stretching from the northeast of Scotland to the southwest of England. Although the new company's corporate headquarters were in Badgerline country at Weston-super-Mare (now in London), the operational headquarters were at Aberdeen. Trevor Smallwood of Badgerline became chairman, and Moir Lockhead of GRT became Deputy Chairman and Chief Executive.

won orders for smaller buses — Dash bodies on Dennis Darts in 1995-6 and AM bodies on Mercedes-Benz 709Ds in 1993; the 1991 709Ds had Reeve Burgess bodies.

Midland had to wait until 1993 for new full-size buses. There were six Mercedes-Benz O.405/Wright that year, followed by a former demonstration O.405 with Alexander body the next year, and in 1994-5 it received 24 Wright-bodied Scania N113s. New minibuses were Merc 709Ds and 711Ds with Alexander or Reeve Burgess bodies.

Top:

For a short time in 1996 the SMT Lothian fleetname was applied to buses in corporate FirstBus style, before the decision was made to simply use the SMT branding. A 1987 Volvo Citybus with Alexander R-type body illustrates the effect.

Above:

Lowland was among the first operators of low-floor buses in Scotland, its early vehicles including this 1996 Scania L113 with Wright Axcess-ultralow body. This bus had a short stay with Lowland, being moved to the new FifeFirst operation in the spring of 1997.

The first external acknowledgement of the new group in Scotland was the appearance of 'Welcome to FirstBus' vinyls in all the buses, but gradually the new FirstBus corporate fleetname style, with the now-familiar 'flying F', appeared on the outside of the fleet. There was talk of a corporate livery, but nothing initially appeared. Instead the Scottish GRT companies changed their own liveries. Grampian's new-generation buses had been delivered in an unusual livery featuring a paler cream and broken green bands that ended in what can only be described as green squiggles. This was the 'GRT Advance' livery, and also found its way on to SMT buses, and (in yellow/green) on Lowland and (in cream/blue) Midland vehicles.

Then Grampian changed its livery, adopting what appeared to be a variation on this as standard. Around the same time the Midland/SMT/Lowland fleets adopted a standard style, with a strong cream base (yellow for Lowland), and green vinyl stripes (blue for Midland).

This signalled a closer relationship between the former GRT companies in central Scotland. Although there were apparently three fleets serving the area between Glasgow and Berwick-upon-Tweed, after April 1996 there were just two, under common management. Midland Bluebird ran services in the traditional Midland area, with depots at Balfron, Bannockburn, Linlithgow and Stirling, and added the western part of the SMT operation, plus depots at Bathgate (Centrex), Livingston and Westfield (Edinburgh).

Lowland expanded west to take in the SMT depots at Dalkeith and Musselburgh, to add to its existing premises at Berwick, Dunbar, Galashiels, Hawick, Jedburgh, Kelso, North Berwick and Peebles. In essence, Eastern Scottish ceased to exist, but the SMT name lives on. Cream/green painted Lowland and Midland buses still carry SMT fleetnames — just SMT, as the Edinburgh and Lothians suffixes were dropped. So Lowland, which had started as a small SBG company hived off from Eastern in 1985, now found itself running much of the old Eastern operation.

The Scottish part of FirstBus was dramatically increased with the purchase in 1996, for £110 million, of SB Holdings, controlling Strathclyde Buses, GCT and Kelvin Central Buses. This former PTE company, with some 1,250 buses, brought with it a mixed fleet. Roundly 70% were double-deckers — Leyland Atlanteans and Olympians, Volvo Ailsas and Citybuses, MCW Metrobuses from the Strathclyde and GCT fleets, Olympians and Metrobuses from the Kelvin fleet. The Kelvin influence also brought Leyland Leopard and Tiger buses, Leyland Nationals and a growing fleet of Volvo B10Ms.

Added to Midland, SMT and Lowland, FirstBus now had a swathe of Scotland stretching from the Clyde to the Tweed, right through the most populous parts of the country. This didn't seem to present a problem when the deal was done, but the Monopolies and Mergers Commission came back early in 1997 and instructed SBH to divest itself of one of its Glasgow depots and the Midland company — the plans had to be in place by the autumn.

Top:
The redrawing of company boundaries in 1996 means that this SMT bus in Haddington is in fact owned by Lowland. It had originally been part of the Eastern Scottish fleet and is a 1984 Leyland Olympian with Gardner engine and Alexander body.

Above:
The Seddon Pennine VII is a fast-disappearing type. The Scottish Bus Group was the only major buyer of the model and the newest are now nearing the ends of their lives. An SMT example with Alexander Y-type bus body heads down Edinburgh's George Street. The stylised diamond logo behind the fleetname predates the ownership of SMT by FirstBus.

Below:
At the start of 1997 a fleet of 13 low-floor Dennis Dart SLFs with Plaxton Pointer bodies were used to replace older buses on a busy cross-city route in Edinburgh. These carry the SMT name, but are owned by Midland Bluebird.

Stagecoach had long been interested in operating services in the Glasgow area. It had started Routemaster services under the Magicbus name in 1986, but sold these on to Kelvin when the SB privatisation seemed imminent. After SB was sold to its management and employees a new company, Stagecoach Glasgow, was set up to compete with Strathclyde. At the eleventh hour a deal was reached, and Stagecoach took a 20% stake in SB Holdings. With the FirstBus takeover, Stagecoach sold its share, but in spring 1997 started up new services in the Glasgow area under the Stagecoach Glasgow name.

This led to a vast influx of new vehicles for the SB fleet, now operating in a rather uninspired all-red livery, as its management snapped up buses from the FirstBus orders and from dealer stock, to respond to the competition.

Other FirstBus competitive activities in 1997 were the setting up of FifeFirst by Lowland, using Scania L113/Wright buses in all-over red to compete on the Edinburgh-Dunfermline-Ballingry corridor with Stagecoach's Fife company, and Kelvin's appearance in Ayrshire, way beyond its normal area, competing with Stagecoach's A1 Service operation.

By mid-1998, six months after the MMC's target date, no divestment had taken place in Glasgow, and the Midland company was still part of the FirstBus group. It was being suggested that FirstBus could argue that there was now, quite demonstrably, competition in Glasgow, so there would be no need to divest. You may know by the time you read this if FirstBus has argued successfully, or if some or all of the divestments have happened.

At the same time we are seeing the first buses in the new FirstBus corporate livery for new lowfloor buses, matching the attractive purple-based interior scheme.

Grampian played an important part in the establishment of FirstBus, now the largest bus operator in Britain, with a total fleet of some 8,000 buses. And Scottish newspapers can still describe it as 'Aberdeen-headquartered'.

Above right:
The simplified livery now being applied to some Scottish fleets lacks the strength of the original GRT-style scheme. A 1980 Seddon Pennine passing the SMT depot in Dalkeith shows the latest look for older vehicles.

Below right:
Strathclyde Buses now trades as Greater Glasgow in an all-over red livery which is the most unimaginative colour scheme ever applied to Glasgow's buses. New to the fleet in 1997 were 50 long-wheelbase Volvo Olympians with 71-seat Alexander Royale bodywork.

Below:
Competition between FirstBus and Stagecoach in 1997 was originally centred on Glasgow but led to the launch of new FirstBus services in Stagecoach territory. FifeFirst is a Lowland-managed operation in the Dunfermline area, while Kelvin has moved to the west of Glasgow to compete with Stagecoach in Ayrshire. Kelvin's Ayrshire buses include 15 Dennis Dart SLFs with UVG UrbanStar bodies, as seen here in Irvine.

COLCHESTER
COLLECTION

Colchester's local buses are in the process of losing their identity, as the new Arriva colour scheme spreads. GEOFF MILLS looks back at the vehicles operated by the erstwhile municipal fleet.

Right:
Colchester Corporation's first diesel buses were five Massey-bodied AEC Regents in 1939. This one was photographed at Parsons Heath in 1953 and survived until 1957.
ALL PHOTOGRAPHS BY THE AUTHOR

Below:
Five Bristol K6As joined the Colchester fleet in 1945, two of which had 56-seat Duple bodies. One of the last survivors is seen in February 1964. It was withdrawn later that year.

Above:
In 1949 Colchester fleet numbers reverted to 1, and 1 to 5 were Daimler CVD6s with Roberts bodies. All five are parked in the undertaking's Magdalen Street garage in 1960. The last were withdrawn in 1968.

Right:
Between 1953 and 1959 Colchester standardised on AEC Regents. The first of these were three Regent IIIs with manual gearboxes and 56-seat Massey bodies.

Top right:
Subsequent deliveries were
Regent Vs, also bodied by
Massey whose works were in
Wigan. A 1957 bus is seen in
Shrub End Estate in January
1967.

Right:
In 1960 Colchester switched to
Leylands, buying Titans with
Massey bodies. This 1963 bus,
one of seven delivered that year,
is seen on its second day in
service.

Bottom right:
In 1972-3 Colchester bought its
first new single-deckers since
1931. These were 15 Bristol
RELL6Ls with Leyland engines and
bodywork built by ECW in
Lowestoft. Massey had by this
time ceased body manufacture,
having been taken over by
Northern Counties. This bus is
seen when new. In later life more
dark red relief was used.

Right:
Small numbers of secondhand buses joined the Colchester fleet in the 1970s and 1980s, including a trio of Tyne & Wear Atlanteans with Alexander bodies. These long-wheelbase buses had nearside staircases — a Newcastle peculiarity — and originally had two doors. For operation in Colchester they were rebuilt as 82-seat single-door buses.

Below:
Colchester introduced coaches to its fleet in 1979, with a pair of Duple-bodied Leyland Leopards. These were 51-seaters with Dominant II bodies which featured deeper windscreens than had been used on the original model.

Left:
The coach fleet was strengthened in 1990 with the delivery of two Dennis Javelins — the first Dennises for 60 years. They had 53-seat Duple 320 bodies and are seen outside Colchester Castle when new. Note the different windscreen layouts. Both Javelins were sold in 1993, following the acquisition of Colchester Borough Transport by British Bus in November of that year.

Right:
Under British Bus, Colchester acquired a number of unusual types transferred from other companies in the group — and usually older than the buses they were replacing. In 1994 seven Leyland National 2s moved south from Midland Fox. They were sold in 1997.

Below right:
The Midland Fox National 2s were replaced by unusual Volvo B10Ms from Grey-Green. These had started life as Plaxton-bodied coaches, but in 1992 were rebodied as buses by East Lancs.

Bottom right:
At the end of 1997 the Cowie Group, successor to British Bus, announced that it was adopting the Arriva name and that a corporate off-white and turquoise livery would be used by all of its subsidiaries. The first Arriva-liveried bus in the Colchester fleet, in December 1997, was an MCW Metrobus transferred from one of the group's London fleets. The Colchester Borough Transport name has been dropped and replaced by Arriva serving Colchester.

Red Rose ROUND UP

A Lancashire review by PETER HESKETH, looking at the changes since deregulation.

The momentous events of the last dozen years within the bus industry have left no part of the country untouched; some, of course, more than others, and Lancashire must be a prime candidate for the area to have witnessed the greatest change, leaving its bus operations changed almost beyond recognition.

The old, pre-1974 County Palatine of Lancaster, as it was then correctly known, abounded in corporation buses. No fewer than 27 undertakings (or 27.25, to be pedantic, as the Mossley part of the SHMD Board was in Lancashire) were in existence 50 years ago, ranging from the might of the Liverpool and Manchester fleets to the minuscule operations of Ramsbottom and Haslingden, running handfuls of buses. Haslingden was the first to disappear, being amalgamated with neighbouring Rawtenstall in 1968 to form Rossendale Joint Transport. Then along came the PTEs in the following year, swallowing up 10 at a stroke: Ashton-under-Lyne, Bolton, Bury, Leigh, Manchester, Oldham, Ramsbottom, Rochdale and Salford to SELNEC (along with the SHMD Board, of course), and Liverpool to Merseyside.

This was company territory too with the BET giant, Ribble present everywhere, or almost. Where it wasn't, North Western, Tilling-owned Crosville and the independent league-leader, Lancashire United, made their respective presences felt, with smaller concerns such as Fishwick and, at one time, the likes of Bamber Bridge Motor Services, Corless, Hart, Naylors, Scout and Viking jealously guarding their own particular patches.

But enough of the history lesson, and forward to more recent times: to be more precise, the eve of deregulation in October 1986. The number of bus operators in the smaller County of Lancashire had declined still further.

Below:
One council bus company that is no more is Lancaster City Transport, which, in turn, had absorbed Morecambe & Heysham in April 1974. A 1957 AEC Regent V/Massey, from the Morecambe & Heysham fleet in its old owner's livery but with its new owner's fleetname, picks up passengers on Morecambe promenade.
ALL PHOTOGRAPHS BY THE AUTHOR

Southport and St Helens were now in Merseyside, whilst Wigan had joined SELNEC's successor, Greater Manchester.

In the 1974 local government reorganisation, Lancaster had absorbed Morecambe & Heysham; Blackburn had likewise absorbed Darwen; and Lytham St Annes, Accrington and the Colne and Nelson part of Burnley, Colne & Nelson had been renamed Fylde, Hyndburn and Pendle respectively. In the north, Barrow-in-Furness had found itself in the nondescript county called Cumbria, and at the opposite end of the old county, Widnes (renamed Halton) and Warrington went into Cheshire.

Lancashire United and the original North Western, both having had their headquarters outside the new Lancashire anyway, had gone, as had all the independents except for Fishwick's, although in 1980 another independent, Border Tours of Barnoldswick, appeared on the scene. Also in that former West Riding town ceded to Lancashire in 1974 was one of the garages of the Gargrave, North Yorkshire operator, Pennine. To complete the scene, at the opposite extreme of the county at Skelmersdale was a garage of the new North Western, the company formed from Ribble's Liverpool area operations a month before deregulation. Ribble was still a National Bus Company subsidiary and very much as it had been since its all-devouring adolescence in the 1920s and 1930s, although the sell-off of NBC was already underway by the time D-day dawned on 26 October.

For many years Ribble had worked closely with other operators in the county. All Fishwick's services were joint

18

with the company, which had also established links with the municipal sector, and by 1986 all the eight municipals had a degree of contact with their NBC neighbour. This ranged from Blackburn's involvement in Lancashire County Council agency schemes, whereby there was no actual joint working but rather a rationalisation of movements along certain corridors, to the joint agreement in Preston. This had commenced in 1948 with the corporation, Ribble and Scout running three joint services, pooling and proportionately sharing the receipts. All this was soon to end with the implementation of the Transport Act. Swept away were those joint agreements and workings; for example, no longer could Hyndburn share income from its Rawtenstall and Blackburn services with its former partners, Rossendale and Blackburn Transports, nor could Blackpool with Fylde.

What was more, the corporation or borough transport departments themselves no longer existed. They were now council-owned bus companies, with their own management boards and assets, supposedly at arm's length from the town halls. Assets were vital and, as will be seen later, the failure to adequately ensure a sufficiency was one company's downfall.

Parallel to all this was the County Council's involvement in the whole scheme of things as the overall co-ordinator of transport in Lancashire, being responsible for the identification of routes deemed to be socially necessary but in need of subsidy. Ironically, new rules meant the end of some good rural initiatives, not the least Ribble's famous Betty's Bus. Working out of Clitheroe garage, a Bristol LH suitably branded and in the care of its regular driver had served many of the more isolated villages in the Ribble Valley since 1980. But in 1986 the routes had to go out to tender and Ribble lost them.

It was this tendering process that was soon to see council company buses in unlikely places, such as Fylde on the former Preston Area Agreement service to Frenchwood, when Preston Bus, as it had become known, registered all its routes commercially except that one. Neighbouring Blackpool Transport found itself on meandering journeys across the Fylde Plain to Preston via Poulton and over Viking's old ground from Great Eccleston. Blackburn gained schools contracts in Burnley, then utilised its resources whilst there to register a route and, as was then common practice, ran buses a few minutes before the established operator, in that case Burnley & Pendle, which also widened its horizons by working tendered services in Manchester. These were but a handful of examples.

Sight was frequently lost of the *raison d'être* of bus operation: to provide a public service. Preston Bus got a kick in the teeth very quickly and it was shocked to realise that it was not just United Transport's mass Zippy onslaught that hurt the most. It was a fact that the public actually liked what was on offer, had little sympathy with the erstwhile corporation transport department and wrote to the local paper to say just that. Preston Bus got its act together, grabbed as many minibuses as it could and wooed back its customers.

Others, unlike United Transport in that they had been around much longer but suddenly similar in outlook, flexed their muscles too. Lancaster was a case in point, especially as it did so in retaliation to a threat to itself. There had been an agency agreement between Lancaster and Ribble, partly funded by the county council, but this came to its inevitable end at the beginning of 1987, whereupon Ribble started running minibuses over some Lancaster routes. Lancaster responded by registering services over Ribble's routes to Preston and Blackpool, and between Blackpool and Preston. Having tasted blood, it then asked Barrow Transport if it would join forces to take on Ribble in Kendal. However, Barrow backed out, leaving Lancaster to set up an out-station. It spread its wings from Kendal as far as Ambleside and secured some tendered work in the Kendal area.

Looking back it is now easier to see how mistakes were made. Some were rectified, helped by circumstances at the time, others were not. Among the former was Blackburn Transport's decision not to commercially register its Outer Circle route. This had been introduced in 1980 in response to local demand, using the ring road to serve Little Harwood, Shadsworth, Witton and Roe Lee. Only days into deregulation, a protagonist in the shape of Greater

Manchester Buses appeared on the scene to work over the route as a tendered service. That could have been GM's foot in the door; soon after, it took over another service Blackburn had failed to register, to Wensley Fold, well inside the borough. Fortunately for Blackburn Transport, GM reappraised its involvement and pulled out of the town. The fact that it was using buses and crews from its Bury garage some 15 miles away was the deciding factor. It was not Blackburn Transport that successfully retendered, but Ribble, considered a preferable stable-mate and less likely than GM Buses to aggressively expand in the town. Whilst this was an example of an interloper from the big league, it is true to say that many more were much smaller, although not necessarily always newcomers.

Mercers of Longridge was an old-established coach firm that started running tendered and commercially registered services around Preston, notably between there and Longridge, competing with Ribble and Preston Bus as far as Gammull Lane, and in the Borough of South Ribble on Fishwick and Ribble routes. These two companies banded

Opposite:
Ribble's large minibus fleet is made up mainly of Alexander-bodied Mercedes, with over 100 being currently in use; one is seen in St Annes carrying Zippy branding. Although the United Transport operation of that name was confined to the Preston area, it is now used throughout Ribble's territory.

Above:
Seen in Burnley, in company with Border Buses vehicles, is a former Hyndburn National Greenway in the Ribble fleet. At this time, the Hyndburn concern had not been fully absorbed and although Ribble fleetnames were carried, the legal lettering still read Hyndburn Transport.

together and eventually bought out Mercer's bus operations, which was a tactic Burnley & Pendle and Pennine had to resort to when Tyrers, another coach operator, from Trawden near Colne, muscled in on the main-line Padiham to Colne route, although not before B&P had introduced its fleet of Eastender Routemasters on to an already bus-saturated corridor. The idea had been to quicken loading times to outdo Tyrers.

The first major change occurred in March 1988, when Ribble became the 63rd NBC subsidiary to be sold. By this time, the company had been trimmed in preparation for sale by losing its Carlisle area operations to Cumberland, and, as already mentioned, those on Merseyside to North Western. Its new owners were a management team headed by Managing Director, Ian Chapman, which soon expanded by buying from United Transport the Manchester-based Bee Line Buzz company in September that year, and shortly afterwards the Zippy operation in Preston and South Ribble.

Above:
Burnley & Pendle, bought by Stagecoach in two stages, still operates a number of older buses including this 1980 East Lancashire-bodied Leyland Leopard, a survivor from a batch of 14. Pending repaint or withdrawal, all B&P vehicles received a Stagecoach vinyl under the fleetname.

Opposite:
A newer bus in the Burnley & Pendle fleet is this Volvo Citybus with Alexander bodywork. Thirteen of this type were placed in service between 1989 and 1991, preceded by two B10Ms with identical bodywork. The B&P fleet was invariably well turned out and electronic destination displays were being fitted to the most modern buses, a process which was continued by the new management.

This ownership of Ribble was to be short-lived, however, as only 12 months later the company was acquired by Stagecoach Holdings. It was Stagecoach, in the guise of Ribble, that was to be the key player in the demise of the first of the eight council-owned companies.

The Government had strongly intimated that such companies should be sold, offering incentives, and Lancaster City Council became the first owning authority to approve, at the end of 1992, the sale of its undertaking (which was no lame duck) by open tender as opposed to a straight sale. As Ribble was the only other major operator in the area, Stagecoach, mindful of the Monopolies and Mergers Commission's likely reaction, did not bid and the Lancaster employees also declined, perhaps foreseeing that sooner or later Ribble would move in anyway.

Realising that after the sale it would have a competitor in its midst, Ribble registered new services over Lancaster's principal routes, in effect attempting to drive it into receivership. Stagecoach then made the City Council an offer (apparently over the odds) for some assets of its company, the garage and 12 of its newest vehicles. Lancaster's coaching arm, Lonsdale Coaches bought in 1988, was sold to Shaw Hadwin of nearby Carnforth. All the staff were made redundant and on 22 August 1993, after 90 years of municipal operation, Lancaster City Transport was no more. All traces were quickly eradicated; Stagecoach reregistered two new Metroriders so that their LCT marks would not linger as reminders of the old company.

Writing in *Buses* in the following month, Lancaster's former Managing Director, Thomas Knowles, observed: 'It may all be in line with the wishes of the government, but it is leading to hardship for dedicated busmen…and ultimately both to a waste of local authority resources and a loss of choice for the passenger. Wasn't that what the 1985 Transport Act was supposed to prevent?'

In the next four years, four of the seven remaining council companies were to be sold, with two, like Lancaster, vanishing altogether.

At the same time as Lancaster City Council was preparing the ground for the sale that never came, Preston Borough Council was going through the complex process of selling its company to its management and staff, the transfer taking place in April 1993. Over 300 Preston Bus employees took up the offer of shares, and all assets, which included the garage in Deepdale, were part of the deal.

In the same year, Fylde Borough Transport was bought

by its management, but this was to be another short-lived situation. Since Lytham St Annes' tramway days, neighbouring Blackpool had had its eyes on the concern. As long ago as 1935 it had made the first of a number of bids, but in 1994 it was successful. Fylde had expanded its operations into Blackpool's territory, not least in the Cleveleys area, and had caused a long-running fares battle on the promenade, with its open-toppers competing with Blackpool's trams and Routemasters. Initially Blue Buses, as the Fylde operation was known, continued as a separate entity, running from its Squires Gate premises. This acquisition of a former council company by a council company is, so far, unique.

In 1995, one of the more enterprising post-1986 newcomers, James of Ormskirk, trading as Little White Buses and running 13 minibuses, was bought out by North Western, and operations in that part of the then British Bus subsidiary's area, serviced by Skelmersdale garage, were rationalised.

The following year, though, was to be a bad year for the council companies in the east of the county, but a good one for Stagecoach Holdings. Firstly, Pendle Borough Council, half owners of Burnley & Pendle, decided after weeks of acrimony culminating in angry scenes at council meetings to sell its share to the highest bidder. Preston Bus and Greater Manchester Buses (North) made offers, but it was, once again, to be Stagecoach that was first past the post. The deal was finalised in January and Burnley Council was outraged, stating that it would never sell its share.

Meanwhile, Hyndburn Council, accepting that its company was desperately in need of the investment it could not afford, offered it for sale. Few showed interest in what had, in reality, become a down-at-heel operation. In 1986 the garage in Ellison Street had not been transferred to the company, unlike elsewhere and, therefore, there was little attraction for prospective buyers. In September, no doubt to the relief of the council, Stagecoach bought the

ageing fleet and what goodwill remained, a sad end to a former tramway operator that not many years before when under the caring wing of the corporation had epitomised, through its resplendent dark blue and red buses, nothing less than civic pride.

Some of the fleet was disposed of, but those taken into stock were painted in corporate stripes with Ribble fleetnames and Hyndburn legal ownership details, until the company was finally wound up the following April, when the garage reverted to the council. Surprisingly, some of the older buses have received Stagecoach livery, not the least a 22-year-old former Preston Atlantean.

In the same month as the Hyndburn sale, Stagecoach had put forward a multi-million pound investment plan for Burnley & Pendle Transport. Burnley Council could not meet its share, unless it cut other council services and, ironically, closed its multi-storey town centre car park, which required urgent and expensive repairs to its concrete structure. Amidst more uproar, it did a U-turn and sold to Stagecoach in November. Another ironic twist was the fact that since the closure of its Burnley garage in 1989, Ribble had out-stationed vehicles at B&P's Queensgate premises, which it now owned.

Before looking at the situation as it is now, it is perhaps useful to review the investment (or lack of it) in new vehicles since 1986. All operators have, to varying degrees, bought new buses and coaches. Ribble has benefited from being part of a major group with a steady flow of new vehicles whilst at the other end of the scale Hyndburn could only manage a handful of minibuses, and National Greenways, and Fylde, after the purchase of its initial minibuses, only bought a pair of new Optare Deltas and secondhand Atlanteans rebodied as single-deckers.

On the other hand, Preston Bus has consistently invested heavily, both in its council days and since privatisation, and its large fleet of Zippy-busting minis is now being replaced. Its last full-sized vehicles were Olympians, bought a year before privatisation. Likewise, Blackburn has embarked on its first-generation mini replacement programme, whilst Blackpool has received double-deckers and supplemented its new minibus intake for the Handybus fleet with eight Optare Excels. They have facilities for wheelchairs and the county council has funded the work on bus-stop improvements.

Rossendale too has taken low-floors, the purchase of East Lancashire Spryte-bodied Dennis Darts for its Rochdale and Bury tendered services being partly funded by Greater Manchester PTE. Its Ellen Smith wing has also had a recent injection of new blood in the shape of a pair of Dennis Javelin coaches. Fishwick has directed its finances towards an ongoing update of the luxury coach fleet and, to a lesser extent, the renewal of its bus stock. Four low-floor Dennis Darts were added in July 1997.

As will have been gathered, Burnley & Pendle's fleet was in need of some investment at the time of the final Stagecoach takeover. Although far from decrepit, its newest buses being three-year-old Metroriders and Volvo Citybuses, a number of Bristol VRTs and Leyland Leopards dating from 1978 were still in regular use and its first minis were ready for retirement. An influx of new Alexander-

bodied Volvo B10Ms and Olympians was therefore welcome in the latter part of 1997.

Putting aside the non-Lancashire operators working into the county and the many smaller ones on tendered routes, the main companies can now be summarised as two major group subsidiaries (Ribble and Burnley & Pendle), three council-owned companies (Blackpool, Blackburn and Rossendale) and three independents (Preston Bus, Fishwick and Border), making eight in total.

For overall management, Ribble and Burnley & Pendle are under the control of Stagecoach North West and, in turn, B&P is managed from Ribble's Preston headquarters. In 1986, B&P had purchased the old-established Padiham coach firm, Viscount Central from Sandown Tours, but as this unit did not sit comfortably within Stagecoach's overall scheme of things it was sold to nearby Border in 1997.

When Stagecoach acquired Burnley & Pendle, it gave the two councils an assurance that services would be maintained for two years. However, there has already been a review of operations, and commercially registered town services in Colne and Barnoldswick and some Nelson area journeys have passed to Border. At the time of writing, the councils were satisfied with the situation, and Pendle expressed pleasure in seeing the promised £2 million investment in new vehicles coming to fruition.

B&P holds a number of county council contracts, and its buses can still be seen well away from Queensgate: in Chipping for example, squeezing through the narrow streets of this attractive village; on its commercially registered Blackpool Flyer express, for which a couple of double-deck coaches are suitably branded; and on its service to Rawtenstall. From early 1997, Ribble (which, it must be remembered, also has a considerable presence outside Lancashire, in Greater Manchester) has not been the Stagecoach operator in the north of the county. That is now Cumberland's privilege, Ribble's Lancaster and Morecambe garages (the latter being the old LCT premises) being transferred to Lancaster & District, a new operation, in February.

Cumberland has, since coming into the Stagecoach fold, advanced steadily southwards. On Barrow's liquidation Ribble had taken over its operations thus expanding its

own area locally, but all its services in the Furness region passed to Cumberland in readiness for the NBC sell-off. Elsewhere in the county, Ribble continues to be very proactive from its headquarters in Frenchwood, Preston and garages at Fleetwood, Blackburn, Chorley and Clitheroe. It has recently introduced a motorway express service between Preston and Nelson to compete with part of North Western Trains' hourly service from Blackpool South to Colne via Preston and Blackburn. This is part of Ribble's intensive inter-urban express network, other aspects of which include Blackpool and Lancaster to Southport and Manchester, and Colne to Manchester.

In Preston, to outdo taxis, it operates evening and later

night services on some of its Zippy turns from the town centre into South Ribble, often replacing minis with double-deckers to cope with the good loadings. The whole Zippy operation in Preston, South Ribble and the Ribble Valley is very lucrative for the company, with 15 services being run all usually using minibuses, but with the three-an-hour Z4 to Longridge being worked by larger Volvo B6s competing with Preston Bus as far as Gammull Lane.

Turning to the council companies, Blackpool finally absorbed its Fylde Blue Buses subsidiary in September 1996, retaining the Squires Gate garage for operations in the south of its area. However, Fylde's Seagull Coaches operation is being scaled down. Blackpool Transport

Services, to give the company its full title, has in the main entrenched back on home ground, concentrating most of its services on the Fylde coast and plain, although it operates some tendered journeys to Preston via Kirkham, and also runs a Sunday limited stop service to Liverpool.

Blackpool is, of course, Lancashire's last remaining tramway operator, being direct owner of the tramcar fleet but not the infrastructure of the system which is still in the hands of the borough council. The ravages of the sea had inflicted irreparable damage to the overhead and threatened the future of the line, but now it has been replaced, funded by Blackpool and Wyre local authorities, Lancashire County Council and the EC.

Above:

Keeping its ageing tramcar fleet on the rails is one of Blackpool Transport's main preoccupations, and many of the prewar trams have been heavily rebuilt. It is hard to imagine that this car started life as an English Electric streamlined railcoach in 1935.

Blackburn, whilst having retreated from destinations such as Harle Syke in Burnley, still maintains one of its early post-deregulation initiatives to a destination farther afield in the shape of its express services to Manchester from its home town and from Clitheroe and, unlike Blackpool, is still very much involved with its coach business. Blackburn Coachlines, as it is branded, not only offers private hire facilities, but a full programme of British

and continental tours, marketed by the company itself through its own travel agency, Blackburn Travel Lines, and glossy, professionally produced brochures.

Inevitably, the company has formed a strong bond with East Lancashire Coachbuilders, whose premises are also in the town. Until recently, it was very much part of the Leyland National Greenway project. All preparatory work to the stripped National bodies, such as cleaning and the fitting of new mechanical parts was done at Blackburn's Intack depot, before return to East Lancashire for finishing. The association has continued with chassis destined for rebodying being made ready at Intack, where the completed vehicles (along with new ones) are eventually Ministry-tested prior to delivery.

Over the hill in the Rossendale Valley, Rossendale Transport is also actively involved in tours and excursions, having acquired the well-known Rochdale company, Ellen Smith. Although the Ellen Smith premises were given up, Rossendale now has another base in Rochdale to maintain a number of Greater Manchester PTE tendered services. It also operates some tendered services in the Burnley area, for which vehicles are out-stationed at the Border premises.

Rossendale's main line, a relic of tramway days between Accrington and Bacup, through Haslingden, Rawtenstall and Waterfoot, was at one time shared with Accrington Corporation and, later, Hyndburn. Now it is extended through Whitworth and on to Rochdale, the Hyndburn share, of course, being Ribble's with Greater Manchester and the Accrington firm, Pilkington's, also having a presence. Of the 36 other services run, most are either hourly or infrequent and one, the X79, is an express from Whitworth to Fleetwood.

A successful innovation has been the Lancashire County Council-subsidised County Rider Rossendale group of routes in Bacup, one of which is a dial-a-ride catering for those who find scheduled services difficult within the County Rider Rossendale area. A three-axle Talbot Express fitted with a wheelchair lift is used.

Now independent, Preston Bus remains much the same as it was in council-owned days, with its 25 services, most intensive, and all within the borough boundary. The Gammull Lane and Farringdon Park routes, for example, both have 6min headways during the day. A lucrative aside is the operation of its programme of excursions using its solitary coach, a Tiger/Duple, bought new at deregulation by the council as an asset adjustment and now, 11 years on, still proving its worth.

The traditional independent, John Fishwick & Sons, also remains very much within the status quo. Nine services are operated, the 111 to Preston via Lostock Hall being its sole preserve and most intensive, with a bus every 15min during the day. Three of the others are the branded FishKwick minibus routes, introduced in 1987 to meet local needs and to stave off any likely Zippy onslaught into the

Leyland part of South Ribble. Its coach fleet is smaller these days, but its tours and inclusive holidays business, like Blackburn's, is still very sound and profitable.

Border Buses, renamed from Border Tours and now well established in Burnley, has, in view of its gain of the former B&P services mentioned, drastically reduced its turns on the main line between Padiham and Colne.

Reference has been made to Lancashire County Council as the transport co-ordinator, and before leaving this overview of the county, it is only right and proper that mention be made of that authority's commitment to public transport. Its production of attractive coloured bus maps and guides for 10 centres of bus operation, supported by comprehensive timetables, are relied on by most operators, including Blackburn and Stagecoach, and is the primary example of that support.

It also conceived and now administers the popular Leisure Links network of routes — the Bowland, Morecambe Bay, Ribble Valley and Lune Valley Ramblers, the Bowland Pathfinder and the Pendle Witch Hopper — running on Sundays and Bank Holidays during the summer from a wide range of points, including Skelmersdale and Darwen. These open up the beautiful Lancashire countryside to those who do not wish to use motor cars.

Some of the services also provide links to the Ribble Valley rail line and the Sunday Dales Rail service from Blackpool over the scenic Settle & Carlisle line, both of which are also subsidised by the county council. On Saturdays, the gap in the line between Clitheroe and Hellifield is bridged by a subsidised coach link. The administration of concessionary fares for the elderly and passes for the disabled are other LCC functions, as is the provision of 15 information centres, the promoting of the Travelwise public transport awareness initiative, and the overseeing of the installation of CCTV in buses to deter and detect vandalism.

On the debit side, though, the county council does appear to have failed to grasp the nettle in one particular area. It supports the park-and-ride principle, its partnership with Preston Borough Council in providing the facility in the Docklands proves this, yet it has not progressed the more grandiose scheme adjacent to the M6 at Red Scar that has featured for a number of years in its Transportation Plan. Access from the motorway has been constructed but the exciting (and feasible) idea of using the track-bed of the old Longridge branch line for a light rail system or a guided busway has not been developed.

Finally, if the question dare be posed, what of the future in Lancashire? There does now seem to be a sensible approach to things, as the transfer of operations between Burnley & Pendle and Border illustrates. Some operators, though, will perhaps continue to be uneasy about their futures. Rossendale has gone on record as saying that it will continue running buses (as Burnley Council did, so adamantly), but now finds itself surrounded by Stagecoach and First Bus.

Preston Bus also now stands alone, but in an additional respect. It is now the sole remaining employee-owned former council concern, and its success could attract predators prepared to put up the vast sum of money needed to buy out its shareholders. It has been suggested that those days could have gone. But, as always, time will, of course, tell.

Above right:
Handyrider is Rossendale's branding for its comprehensive network of minibus routes, for which large numbers of new and second-hand MetroRiders were acquired. This one was bought new in 1986 and is seen in Rawtenstall bus station, adjacent to the undertaking's Bacup Road garage.

Right:
The splendour that was once Hyndburn, depicted by an East Lancashire-bodied Leyland Titan PD3A/1, new in 1962. Areas of grey, that with age looked like primer, were later added to the distinctive dark blue and red livery. Hyndburn, investment-starved and down-at-heel, was bought by Stagecoach in 1996.

LEOPARDS
A Naturalist's Guide

The Ancestor *(P.Pardus Originalis)*

The Leopard was first glimpsed in Liverpool in 1926 when a pair was delivered to the local corporation. The Leopard LSG2 *(Panthera Pardus Originalis)* was really a long-wheelbase Lion with 38-seat bodywork on a 197in wheelbase forward control chassis. It was powered by a 6.5-litre petrol engine although many felt it was no fleeter across country than the 5.1-litre-engined Lion. If this pair had bred then *Originalis* would have been the progenitor of a later genus of underpowered long-wheelbase Leopards, but instead the line died out and so our story moves forward to the 1950s.

Darwinian Evolution

In the later part of that decade a gap opened up in the normally comprehensive Leyland product range. Underfloor-engined single-deckers had been represented in the domestic range by the Royal Tiger, Olympian, Olympic and Tiger Cub but by 1957 only the last was still offered. Within the maximum 30ft by 8ft dimensions then permitted, its lowly 110bhp was sufficient for stage work amongst traffic also considerably less quick off the mark than today, whilst express coach services ran along slow-moving trunk roads and through congested town centres, making high average speeds impossible. The opening of the first motorways rapidly altered this situation, Midland Red in particular developing turbocharged coaches capable of an 80mph cruise. In this new market the Tiger Cub was clearly inadequate and so in 1959 Leyland sired the Leopard L1 bus *(P. Pardus Boxus)* and L2 coach *(P. Pardus Luxus)*. These were fundamentally Tiger Cub frames but fitted with the O.600 engine instead of the O.350 or O.375, giving the L2 a dizzy 130bhp at 2,200rpm for sustained hard work — both the mileage

The Leopard (*Panthera Pardus*) was once a common sight in the landscape, but is now being hounded to extinction by changes to its environment and the failure of its bloodline. OLIVER HOWARTH wanders off into the undergrowth to trace the main members of this fascinating branch of the big cat family.

Above:
Classic Leopard. A new North Western Leopard L2 on tour in Scotland in 1965, with Harrington's classic Grenadier body. The Leopard offered more relaxed touring than the smaller-engined Tiger Cub which it ultimately replaced. North Western took a pair of L2s in 1965.
SJB

Below:
Dual-purpose Leopard. The BET group was quick to take advantage of the new 11m-length limits and PSU3 Leopards were soon running for a number of its subsidiaries, generally with this style of bodywork. This is a Hebble vehicle in Blackpool in 1962.
Harry Hay

between overhauls and average speed rose whilst a Leopard coach was a ton lighter than the over-engineered 8-ton Royal Tiger (*P. Tigris Rex*, hunted to extinction by cost accountants in 1954 after mauling a series of fuel bills). As a result, the Leopard was able to meet new road conditions and financial expectations in the aftermath of the lightweight bus escapades.

The L2 also had drop frame extensions to support a luggage boot and an optional two-speed Eaton rear axle and from 1961 air suspension was available, although a series of bellows failures eventually led to a reversion to leaf springing on the vehicles involved. At launch, Western SMT immediately took 20 leaf-sprung L2s with 30-seat Alexander bodies, which were capable of 16mpg on the Anglo-Scottish services — at a time when most of the journey was made at 40mph. This was an important sale as the AEC Reliance 470 was already established in Scotland and the evolution of the Leopard was in some ways a response to the menacing posture of Southall. Indeed the Scottish Bus Group, as it became, would influence the Leopard range for many years.

The Leopard Grows Up

The L1, with slightly derated engine (125bhp), found popularity in the Irish Republic, CIE taking 170 between 1961 and 1963, which they bodied as 45-seat buses. Left-hand drive versions (*P. Pardus Sinistra*) found favour in Portugal where the LHL1 was a successful coach. However, the change to UK Construction and Use Regulations in 1961 led to bodies on the L1 and L2 growing to 31ft or thereabouts

and sporting curved windscreens for the first time, whilst a maximum dimension variant was launched measuring 36ft by 8ft 2½in with an 18ft 6in wheelbase but tighter steering lock to maintain the existing swept turning circle. At this point, for the first time we meet the gremlin dwelling behind the Faringdon Works boilerhouse who allocated the chassis codes, because whilst this variant might have been expected to be the L3 or LL1/ LL2, instead it capriciously became the PSU3.

BET Standards (*P. Pardus Tinflorus*)

Big orders were placed by Midland Red, Ribble and several other BET subsidiaries for buses and dual-purpose vehicles carrying the later, curved-windscreen BET style of bodywork complete with flooring seemingly made from a thin sheet of tin which allowed all the passengers to enjoy the throaty snort of a Leopard working hard — and sometimes to savour the smells as well if the large floor traps didn't fit too well. In my experience, Midland Red was not averse to driving Leopards into a depot midway along one of their lengthy interurban routes, to let a fitter hoick open the traps and tinker with the tickover, then rev the engine hard and asphyxiate the patient passengers. Those long interurban expresses had another problem as well, as I found when aboard a 12-year-old Leopard. One moment we were bowling through the verdant Worcestershire countryside in early evening sunlight; next we had spluttered to a stop three miles from my destination on the last journey of the day. Someone really should have fitted bigger fuel tanks to vehicles clocking up those daily mileages — the driver wasn't even surprised. Disgusted, but not surprised. And as the church clock tolled the knell of parting day, I would have given much for a sight of a double-decker wandering slowly o'er the lea. Fat chance, boy, so pick up your suitcase and walk.

Reliable McLeopards *(P. Pardus Caledonius)*

The PSU3 did especially well in Scotland, where, teamed with the Alexander Y-type, it was an immediately successful and convincing design. The first one went to Edinburgh with no less than three very high entrances, representing the last fling of the late-1950s wave of standee experiments; but it was SBG (and especially Central SMT) who fell in love with the Y-type-bodied Leopard. In 1971 Leyland deleted the manual transmission option except for the PSU3.3R, which continued in production until 1978 for the Scottish Bus Group only, with examples ending up running for all seven subsidiaries. By then, not only were new vehicles going into service replacing almost identical old Leopards, but Alexander's factory yard was swarming with a backlog of chassis that tended to get coach or bus bodies without anyone checking the exact specification of the hardware underneath. As a result, there were some very underpowered coaches and intractable buses running around Scotland until the engineers were able to swap the relevant bits and restore some Scottish common sense. Ho hum hoots.

None the less, the SBG loved its Leopards. Indeed the legendary toughness of Lanarkshire housewives owes much to their training on generations of Leyland-built mobile assault courses; and long after SMT had become KCB, an evening stroll round one of their depots (or as I prefer to think of it, Shotts In The Dark) would reveal a battered, bloodied but not totally bowed pride of Leopards being got ready to start another day's hunting on the Monklands plains at sunrise. Listen to those drums, bwana. Is it the Zulus? The Mau Mau? Or just The Bay City Rollers?

Have Big Cat, Will Travel

In the 1960s the model enjoyed considerable success abroad as well: CIE took 273 PSU3s; New Zealand took 232 air-suspended short PSU3s (35ft long) ordered in 1966 with beefy 155bhp O.680 engines; and sizeable quantities went to Denmark, Finland, the Netherlands, Australia, Argentina, Portugal and the Dominican Republic. In the late 1960s, big orders came from Ulsterbus and from CIE (for Van Hool-bodied coaches); 193 Leopards were released into the wild in Kinshasa, Congo; whilst the delivery of 745 to the Department of Government Transport, New South Wales, made DGT the biggest Leopard tamer of them all.

Interestingly, it would appear that none at all was sold to Germany, which is probably quite lucky as it has saved all sorts of confusion. German Leopards *(P. P. Jagdpanzer)*, whilst clearly ideal at getting past roadblocks of French lorry drivers in the course of a quick dash across country to the Calais hypermarkets, are sadly lacking in passenger comforts. And anyone who has tried flagging down a main battle tank can tell you how wearing that can be. Despite all the provocations, Stagecoach has so far resisted the temptation to import any of these…

Above:

Luxurious Leopard. When new to Southdown, this Leopard with Duple Commander IV body was the last word in luxury, even if it did look dated by the time it was photographed running for Hants & Dorset in 1980. The location is Cheltenham's busy coach station, a popular meeting place for Leopards and other lesser breeds.

Oliver Howarth

The Short Leopard (*P. Pardus Brevis*)

Also in 1964, the PSU4 replaced L1/L2; it made maximum use of PSU3 components but with a short 16ft 2in wheelbase, to give a vehicle with dimensions of 31ft 4in by 8ft 2½in. However, the last Ls were not delivered until the end of 1966 (mainly to fleets who ran Tiger Cubs rather than Leopards and wanted to standardise on parts). The PSU4 was also popular as some fleets had agreements with the Unions that one-man-operation was permissible on buses seating no more than 45; Ribble even had some PSU3s delivered as very spacious 45-seat buses until this rule was renegotiated, after which an extra eight seats were pushed in. Shorter coaches also became popular with some big fleets where their capacity was competitive with the Bedfords beloved of private hirers. This was a fairly short-lived trend, but as late as 1976 Wallace Arnold's Devon fleet took three narrow-bodied PSU4s for wriggling over Dartmoor and these enjoyed very long lives, including a mid-life rebodying.

By the late 1970s, small vehicles and rural routes seldom mixed and the PSU4 was no more, the Bristol LH and B-series National catering for most needs. But in search of a 9m midi, Western SMT sliced two L-registered Y-types down to what we would now call Dart size for operating a restricted route in Dumfriesshire in 1979, creating the briefest Leopards of all.

Back to Front (*P. P. Standus Maximus*)

So by the mid-1960s the Leopard was a roaring success, especially in rural and interurban bus roles, but the urban market was evolving and Leyland's engineers carried out drastic surgery to produce the Panther in 1964;

Above:
Fast Leopard. Midland Red bought Leopards for interurban operation, including 50 PSU3s with Marshall bodywork in 1974. One is seen loading in Pool Meadow, Coventry, in the ownership of Midland Red South in 1987.
SJB

Right:
Faster Leopard. For most of the 1970s the Leopard was the standard National Express coach, initially in 11m form, later in the maximum length 12m PSU5 variant. Most had bodies by Duple or Plaxton, but this odd beast has Willowbrook's short-lived Spacecar body. Seen in Leicester in the ownership of Midland Red South, the destination blind is giving would-be travellers the option of destinations at opposite ends of England — Whitehaven or Weymouth. A windscreen sticker confirms the latter.
SJB

The 51-seat dual-door PSU3.1R *(P. P. Standus Maximus)* was briefly tried by some in 1968 — three bodied by Massey going to Caerphilly, four by East Lancs to Southend plus five similar vehicles for Barrow — giving a similar layout to the Panther and a very high capacity, but with seven-league steps due to the high frame and underfloor engine. This is a concept that was popular on the Continent for far too long as anyone struggling onto a 1970s' Renault in Paris or a DAF in Rotterdam will have found. Silcox of Pembroke Dock went one better (indeed 11 better) with a Derwent saloon seating 62 in 36ft, also in 1968. With the reduction of vehicle choice in the mid-1970s, LUT took a small batch of dual-door Derwent-bodied PSU3s as its previously favoured chassis types

here many of the Leopard running units were used in a new frame with the engine moved to the rear overhang to give what Leyland claimed was excellent weight distribution. The Panther *(Neofelis Nebulosa)* suffered from insufficient development (not unlike many of our post-deregulation buses) and although it was an excellent driver's bus, it needed more time over the pits than was healthy.

A handful of operators, seeing the high capacity of the Panther as a plus but viewing the undoubted unreliability of the first-generation rear-engined saloons as a minus, tried to get the same result with indestructible Leopards.

(the Bristol RE, LH and Seddon RU) had all been deleted, found wanting, or both; however the awkward exit meant that these were unpopular vehicles, sold out of service by GMT many years before the single-doored members of the same batch were retired.

Bus Grant Coaches *(P. P. Porta Maximus)*
Three factors gave the Leopard a new lease of life at the start of the 1970s: the extending motorway network, the introduction of bus grant and a change in coach buying so major dealers purchased large batches for stock. As a result, sales rose by 200 a year in Britain to over 500 in

Above:

Bus Leopard. Outside the Scottish Bus Group most urban fleets in the 1970s were buying rear-engined buses with two-step entrances and a relatively low floor. But some fleets preferred the proven reliability of the Leopard, even if it did mean a three- or four-step entrance. Chester City Transport was one of those, taking Leopard buses with bodies by Northern Counties, as seen here, and Duple.
SJB

Above left:

Dull Leopard. NBC took Willowbrook's Spacecar concept and watered down the specification to produce the dull 003. The Spacecar had distinctive windscreens and a stylish little kick-up in the waistline at the rearmost side window. NBC was having none of that frippery. This 1979 Devon General Leopard was the prototype of a sizeable batch of 003s delivered in 1980. Carrying route branding for the Mayflower Express linking Torquay and Plymouth, it appears to have wandered a long way from its native habitat in this view outside London's Victoria Coach Station.
SJB

Left:

Exotic Leopard. In later years Leopard coaches appeared in Britain with continental bodywork. The main builders were Caetano and Van Hool. This Limebourne Coaches Leopard has a Van Hool body.
SJB

1972. There was also a significant switch from low spec buses to higher spec chassis, using the horizontal version of the O.680 engine (which only came with the pneumocyclic gearbox). Throughout the 1970s, bus grant coaches with jack-knife doors were popular with a wide range of operators. Inspired by a Plaxton Sales Manager, Charles Marshall, who went on to be Managing Director of OK Motor Services (which came to use large numbers of the type), these looked just like coaches to the passengers, but qualified for 25% bus grant (50% from 1971 until the end of Leopard production) by reason of their modified entrances. Hence in 1973, OK Motor Services was able to trade in a pair of two-year-old Reliance coaches for similar but brand new bus grant Leopards and receive a cash credit for the transaction. It didn't take long for this offer to assure the type's popularity, Barton Transport being the biggest exponent, replacing its entire fleet with over 300 Plaxton-bodied Leopards and Bedfords. However it was important for the bus grant vehicles to spend at least 25% of their mileage on stage work and if an operator overlooked this for a while, it could explain a sudden flurry of coaches running urban bus routes.

Longer Leopards (P. P. Maximus)

The 12m Leopard was first seen in 1970, the first prototype going to CIE which liked it enough to order 212 more fitted with stylish MetSec bodywork. Redesigned suspension with resilient mounts gave the 20ft-wheelbase PSU5 a better ride whilst the chassis was beefed up, the Worldmaster front axle fitted, and a 10-speed splitter gearbox offered. However, sales were slow as the completed vehicle cost 10% more for the gain of just four extra seats (7.5% more revenue if every seat was filled) and it was not until the ending of bus grant that buyers got seriously interested in high capacity vehicles for school journeys. Also, the gremlin mentioned earlier ensured that the PSU5 chassis codes were kept out of synchronisation with the shorter models (which were by now the PSU3B and PSU4B); as a result the codes for the 12m model always trailed two letters behind the codes for its older brethren.

Greasy Bits (Viscera)

In the 1970s, the chassis code gremlin really got cracking, with a range of fairly small-scale changes resulting in a shower of different variants. The PSU3A/PSU4A used the rationalised version of the pneumocyclic gearbox but were replaced, in October 1970, by the PSU3B/PSU4B on which the original Eaton rear axle was replaced by the ex-AEC Reliance unit which allowed bigger brakes to be fitted. Late 1974 saw the PSU3C/PSU4C/PSU5A with spring brakes, auto slack adjusters, water-cooled air compressor and modified engine mountings. Late 1976 brought the PSU3D/PSU4D/PSU5B with a heavier spring option for luxury bodies carrying toilet and galley. The five-speed box became standard, the four-speed remaining only as an option, whilst only months later, in spring 1977, these models were superseded by the PSU3E/PSU4E/PSU5C

with the air-brake reservoirs mounted further back to reduce the incidence of accident damage. (Incidentally I must at this point pay a special acknowledgement to Doug Jack's masterwork, The Leyland Bus [Omnibus Leylandii] without which no overview of Leopards would be complete.)

Although in engineering terms the breed was evolving, to the passenger the Leopard still looked, felt and sounded the same: noisy, a little bit ponderous and a little bit out-of-date. So far as the driver was concerned, vagaries of production, coupled with that famous Leyland quality control, tended to leave pedal settings a bit of a lottery, erring towards over-heaviness, whilst the steering had been a bicep builder until the introduction of well-developed power steering transformed the Leopard's willingness to be pointed in the right direction, making it a pleasure to drive on the motorway. Which was timely, as this was to become its prime habitat.

The Snow Leopard (P. Uncia)

From its formation in 1972, National Express became a major buyer of Leopard coaches. Having inherited a large fleet of Leopards from its NBC operators, most carrying Panorama or Commander bodywork (P. P. Triplexum), a double-glazed M-type was built as a would-be progenitor of a new breed for National Express, but this was not deemed successful although a dozen more were built later for SBG. Instead, Plaxton, Duple and Willowbrook supplied suitably sparse variants of their mainstream models. In 1977, to take a year at random, NBC took 200 Leopards — 27 PSU5, 2 PSU4 and 171 PSU3 — and none of them was bodied as a bus. Instead they filtered into fleets in all-white or the half-and-half local coach schemes, in some cases being chosen by fleet engineers who wished to stem the inexorable march of the Leyland National onto NBC's interurban bus routes.

Willowbrook's 002, built on 10 Leopards for Tyneside PTE in 1972, was too bus-like for National Express but was followed by the 008 Spacecar (The Spirit of Adventure) and then the NBC inspired 003 (The Broken Spirit); and when Willowbrook folded, NBC took the same charmless concept to ECW who built the B51 (The Spirit of Coaching Past). Although the alternate rows of red and blue seats were dropped, 'rosewood' Formica was still considered a pretty trendy interior by someone in the Buying Office right up until the end of deliveries. Local coaches did even worse, as Tilling Five Year Plan moquettes continued to be specified for stage work into the 1980s.

As a result of the factors mentioned above, by 1975 most Leopards were being built as coaches. Both PTEs and municipals started to take numbers of coaches for private hire and light stage work, whilst for pure coaching, Van Hool, Jonckheere and Caetano imports did well with independents who wanted to go one better than Smiths Happiways.

Urban Leopards (P. P. Urbanis)

Municipal fleets, in particular, saw solid virtues in the Leopard and Nottingham took over 30, mostly with bus seats in Dominant coach shells for an optimistic Park & Ride venture — many were sold off quickly after council expectations about the transfer of custom from car to bus were not met. Lancaster took 31 in the late 1970s in a clear-headed, fast-track, fleet replacement scheme following the merger of two of the most life-expired fleets in the country. The first 26 were all Y-types (Duple building the last five as Alexanders were too busy) with a mix of bodies, all modified to T. W. W. Knowles' requirements with a wider entrance allowing four-leaf doors to be fitted. Western SMT and Roy Marshall at Burnley & Pendle followed suit — but Central SMT ground on with narrow doors and manual transmission until 1980, when it finally accepted delivery of examples with pneumocyclic gearboxes. By this time bus bodies were changing, and the Duple Dominant was winning many new sales as production of the Y-type and the BET-derived Plaxton Derwent and Willowbrook designs tailed off.

Coaches and Hot Air (P. P. Hypocaust)

In 1979, with the big-hearted Reliance dropped from the range, a ZF synchromesh variant of the Leopard was announced to mop up the remaining loyal (and prestigious) AEC user base. The PSU3F/PSU5D had a six-speed ZF shift, power steering, a tachograph instead of a speedometer and a further uprating of the chassis. Both the best known AEC buyers took examples — 10 for Premier Travel and eight for Yelloway, whose notoriously tough Devon services had seen the rival Volvo demonstrator blow its engine after four days (or so the Rochdale operator's chief engineer told me not long afterwards). However, the coach market was now moving faster, and staunchly conservative Yelloway was considering Neoplans for its future needs even before acquisition by Carlton PSV. Going with the flow, Duple announced the Dominant III body for SBG, which dressed the mutton as lamb (or was it a sheep in wolf's clothing?) and Go Whittle took five similar Leopards for London express work, although Eastern Scottish decided to wait for the arrival of something new from the Leyland Zoo.

The deregulation of coaching in 1980 lay behind such heresy, opening the express routes to competition and shifting the dwindling excursion market, based on licensed pick-up points, towards packaged holidays which majored on service and style to differentiate one company from another. Suddenly coaches had to be big and sleek,

Above:
Urban Leopard. The Scottish Bus Group was the biggest user of Leopard buses. They could be found the length of the country and on all types of operations. A Clydeside Leopard heads towards the urban jungle that is central Glasgow on a cross-city service in 1987. Like most SBG Leopards it has an Alexander Y-type body.
SJB

Below:
Nine lives? Well, two certainly. This Leopard started life in 1974 with Weardale Motor Services, at which stage it had a Plaxton body. It was rebodied for further service by East Lancs, and is seen in Bishop Auckland in 1997.
Oliver Howarth

Opposite:
Bright Leopard. The yellow and cream livery of Alexander (Northern) adds a splash of colour to the granite buildings of Aberdeen. This Leopard has a Duple Dominant body.
SJB

with videos, hostess serveries, flush toilets and enough luggage space for a hundred suitcases; suddenly a Leopard was no longer Supreme but looking somewhat long in the fang. A high floor and 250bhp was the only game in town.

Of course by the time all the resultant highly specified ironmongery was five years old, it was unfit for most purposes, incapable of being cascaded, and in consequence depreciated like a house falling off a cliff. But long before the virtues of multipurpose coaches were being appreciated anew, the Leopard was a back number.

The Law of the Jungle *(P. Pardus Senex)*
In 1979 Leopard production was transferred to LAPland, the new truck works outside Leyland nominally built for the T45 Roadtrain, but it returned to its ancestral home, Faringdon Works, in 1981 for what proved to be the last year of production. Another variant (PSU3G/PSU5E) saw the O.680 rationalised so that it had more in common with the TL11 and the previous 175bhp output was raised to 185bhp. An O.690-engined prototype had been tried in 1979 and a TL11 was fitted to a 1978 Leopard of Wallace Arnold, but the writing was on the wall and at the 1980 Motor Show the Leyland B43 was announced, soon to be named the Tiger at a lavish launch in Morocco. The Leopard, it was stated, was to remain in production as long as there was a demand.

Nationals and National 2s were the UK's standard saloon by now, even being bought by the once sceptical SBG, as increasingly the virtues of mechanical simplicity were overtaken by considerations of passenger comfort; and the last SBG Leopards entered service in 1982 wearing Y plates. Other late customers included the Ministry of Defence, who took 19 Wadham Stringer Vanguards; whilst 10 were built for the New Zealand

market with three axles to comply with restrictive axle limits — they received 12.3m coachwork.

Meanwhile, a 170bhp variant of Tiger was announced early in 1982 to replace the Leopard bus. New coach models were flooding in and in the summer of 1982 European legislation killed the Leopard; the last ones entered service in 1983.

Cats With More Than One Life *(P. Pardus Meccano)*
It should be clear by now that although a fleetlist may have shown a rash of different Leopard designations in the same fleet, many non-standard variants would also have been created as hard-pressed fitters used whatever brake parts, axles or air tanks fell to hand and could be bodged to fit. Independent of Horsforth went one further by rebuilding a 10m model as an 11m rear-engined Leopard coach, although the reasoning behind this project is unclear even after several pints of Tetley's.

The Leopard chassis was especially favoured by rebodiers in later years. Lack-lustre ECW bodies of the early 1970s with drooping, unsupported boots were replaced with shiny new Duple coachwork for GMT. The ECW body removed from one of this batch was bought by Holmeswood of Rufford and fitted onto another old Leopard chassis, ex-Midland Red, to create a vehicle of non-pedigree status — or 'a right old mongrel', as we say in Lancashire.

Willowbrook and East Lancs built up a small industry rebodying Leopards after deregulation, the Lynx-like Warrior in particular finding new buyers for Leopard service buses, whilst Plaxton rebodied a number of Leopards as coaches for a dealer. On a slightly different tack, CIE left the bodywork on its 200-odd M-class Leopards untouched, but rebuilt them with an eclectic mix of GM *(P. P. Gasguzzlus)*, DAF or Cummins engines.

37

However, the Leyland O.680 engines removed from the M class did live on in other vehicles, a proceeding which with hindsight seems a little odd, especially as this was the part of the vehicle which other operators trusted most.

European Wildcat (*Felis Silvestris*)

The Leopard had already spawned imitators — SBG, seeking engineering minimalism in the early 1970s, had asked Seddon to build a Gardner-powered Leopard substitute, with one frame member being cranked around the bulky 6HLXB — and several hundred examples of the resulting Pennine VII entered service. Although the manual gearbox variant was memorably described by a leading (English) busman as 'only suitable for ploughing', it was undoubtedly a sensible coach once out of the city limits, and the semi-automatic variant in retrospect looks to have been a good, solid bus that was strangely ignored outside Scotland. Later on, SBG went further and persuaded Dennis to produce another Gardner-engined Leopard, the Dorchester, rather than force poor, misunderstood Central to use comfortable, modern Tigers for stage service work; and today, maintaining the Scottish connection, Stagecoach has realised the usefulness of heavyweight underfloor-engined chassis capable of a decent turn of speed and has purchased large numbers of mid-engined B10Ms (*Felis Silvestris*). Anyone who has seen the Alexander PS-bodied examples storming into Blackwood bus station or rumbling out of Dunfermline bound for Glasgow will recognise that here we have the true successor to the Leopard of 30 years ago.

The Last Leopards

Leyland gave birth to a remarkably adaptable genus in 1959, yet, incredible though it is to someone who grew up in a world where every other bus was some pard or other, the Leopard has now outlived its normal life expectancy. As I write, independent operators still have a number in service but all the major operators are withdrawing their final examples — even in Scotland.

Hopefully there is one place where Leopards will find a last sanctuary. High in the inaccessible mountains of County Donegal, the species is still vigorous. Some day, inevitably, civilisation will reach these hills and teach the natives about using converted parcel vans on rural bus routes. But I, for one, have no intention of despoiling their older, simpler way of life.

Let us hope that *Panthera Pardus* will still be sighted in its natural habitat by keen observers for many years to come.

Note to scholars: Some of the Latin names in this article are zoologically correct, whilst others are deliberately puerile (from *puerilis*).

Leopards' graveyard. A group of dead and dying Leopards being cannibalised at the Kirkintilloch depot of Kelvin Central in 1990. The five buses in the dark red livery of Central Scottish were new in 1977. The Leopard in Kelvin Scottish colours — fifth from the camera — is in fact a 1965 vehicle which has been rebuilt as a breakdown truck. Oliver Howarth

CAPITAL COLOUR

Until the mid-1980s virtually every local bus service in London was run by a red bus. Route tendering changed all that, adding both colour and vehicle variety, as STEWART J. BROWN describes.

For some 25 years — from the start of the 1960s to the middle of the 1980s — London's buses offered little variety to the enthusiast. The centre of the capital was served by masses of red double-deckers. RTs slowly gave way to Routemasters. After a brief flirtation with standee single-deckers the Fleetline appeared and soon started to disappear.

The hapless Fleetlines were followed by Titans and Metrobuses — both types still with us — but wherever you went in Greater London, buses were red. It was as if it had been ordained: as if there had in fact been an 11th commandment which Moses had thrown away because it didn't make much sense at the time: 'All London buses shall be red.' The only real variety was the occasional overall advert.

There was colour in London before LRT tendering, with a very few routes being run by independent operators with the authorisation of London Transport. One such was Continental Pioneer which ran from Richmond station to the top of Richmond Hill. In 1979 it was running an ex-London Transport RF-class AEC Regal IV. ALL PHOTOGRAPHS BY THE AUTHOR

London Transport was a huge organisation. In 1980 its bus fleet totalled 6,481 vehicles, according to *The Little Red Book*. And, in the manner of most big organisations, it had a certain lumbering momentum. A bit like a super-tanker. Once it got going it kept going; a change of direction wasn't something to be done quickly. Indeed, at LT it wasn't something to be done at all.

As well as being big and slow to change, LT had a monopoly of bus services in Greater London. In the political climate of the mid-1980s, the very idea of a monopoly was a bit like waving a red rag to a bull — or in this case a red bus to a true-blue Tory. Indeed many of us free-thinkers marvel that the popular board game of the same name wasn't outlawed, as Conservatives got more and more het up in the pursuit of the holy grail: competition.

Deregulation had undeniably reinvigorated the coach business in 1980. It had shaken National Travel out of its lethargy. It was clearly A Good Thing, and that is why it was about to change the bus business too. But even the most avid free-market Conservatives drew back from deregulating London's buses. And so it came to pass in 1986 that while cities such as Manchester and Glasgow got transport chaos, London got route tendering. Deregulation was to follow.

Out would go high-cost LT red buses, from April 1985 owned by the newly-created London Buses Ltd. In would come flexible low-cost responsive private sector entrepreneurs. Well, private sector entrepreneurs, certainly. Low-cost, yes. But flexible and responsive? Well…maybe not. Responsibility for the London route network would remain with London Regional Transport, so there wouldn't be that much flexibility. Nor the sort of prompt response to changing circumstances that would characterise the deregulated bus market outside London.

But there would be colour, and lots of it. A generation of Londoners who had assumed that God had decreed all buses would be red was in for a shock.

Above left:
After starting up with secondhand Fleetlines, London Buslines bought new Leyland Olympians. In 1990 it took 17 with Northern Counties Palatine bodies.

Left:
In its early days on London tendered routes, Metrobus used three unusual Bedford YMTs with Wadham Stringer Vanguard bodywork. They were bought new in 1986.

Opposite:
Sampson's used ex-London DMS-class Fleetlines on its tendered service in Enfield, one of which is seen here in 1987 passing in front of a more traditional London bus.

Opposite inset:
Eastern National expanded quickly in London and was soon running Bristol VRTs on tendered routes. This one is seen in Enfield after the creation of Thamesway and carries its new owner's fleetname.

Reasonably enough, LRT started the route tendering process in the suburbs. Had the whole thing proved to be unworkable, the last thing LRT wanted was a major problem in the West End. Thus the first independent to take over a former London Buses service under the new tendering arrangements — on 13 July 1985 — was Len Wright with route 81 operating between Hounslow and Slough. Len Wright was a respected coach operator, and had been involved in providing high-specification coaches for pop groups.

The 81 was launched under the London Buslines name using ex-London Fleetlines, demonstrating that while the workings of the Fleetline were way beyond the ability of LT, they were not too daunting for an independent. London Buslines would expand over the following decade and it would do this with new buses — Leyland Lynxes and Olympians, and Mercedes-Benz minibuses. Five L-registered Olympians for London Buslines were destined to be the last new Leyland buses for London. The company's livery would improve too, under the direction of Best Impressions in 1990. London Buslines ultimately operated as part of Len Wright's Q Drive group and was taken over by CentreWest in 1996.

London Buslines' yellow Fleetlines weren't the only splash of colour in suburban London on that July day. Two National Bus Company subsidiaries also won tendered routes — Eastern National and London Country. The only other independent to take over an LT route in 1985 was Crystal of Orpington which won the lightly-used 146 in Bromley.

Quite clearly the routes lost by London Buses were the ones which attracted most attention, with their new operators, new liveries and in some cases unusual vehicles. These included Eastern National's Bedford YMQ-S midis with Wadham Stringer bodies in Enfield, and Lex-bodied Leyland Cubs operated by Crystal. However London Buses won tenders too, retaining six of the routes which were up for grabs in 1985.

and also got rather closer to the centre than most other tenderers with the Hampstead Hoppa, operated by Mercedes minis. This was of course the period of fanciful names: Hoppas, Shoppas, Skippers, Clippers, Nippers, Sprinters, Shuttles, Hoppanstoppers (I'd like to say I made that one up, but I'm afraid it's genuine) and even Wee Happy Buses (as opposed to Big Miserable Buses, but with a name like that, obviously not in London). London went in for Hoppas in a big way.

Some new — and more down-to-earth — names appeared on LRT routes in 1986. Metrobus of Orpington, which already operated services from Croydon, started to expand, initially with ex-LT Fleetlines. Metrobus would become a major force in the southeast corner of London, later buying new Dennis Darts and Optare Excels, new and used Olympians, and a few Lynxes. But there was never a Metrobus Metrobus, if you know what I mean.

Ensign Bus, a company which had come to prominence as a dealer in ex-London Fleetlines, took over a service in Dagenham in 1986 which was to be the foundation of a sizeable network in the east of the capital. It started with ex-London Fleetlines — now there's a surprise — but by 1988 it was buying its first new buses for an LRT tendered service: these were Metrobus IIs, an unusual choice for an independent.

Cityrama, a tour operator, joined the growing band of ex-LT Fleetline operators in 1986 when it took over a service in south London — Suburbarama? It eventually had two routes, but lost both on retendering in 1988-9. Sampson of Hoddesdon took some routes in the Enfield and Waltham Cross areas, with a particularly unusual livery — blue and maroon. Sampson's business was acquired by County Bus & Coach in 1989. Also to the north, the Potters Bar local service was taken over by North Mymms Coaches.

Scancoaches broke new ground in 1986 by taking over a contract to which it introduced new buses — Jonckheere-bodied Scanias — the first time this had been done by an independent. These were the first — and last — Jonckheere bus bodies to be sold in the UK. The Scanbus fleetname was used for this operation, which served Shepherd's Bush — or even Schepherd's Bush, if you were to believe the destination blinds which were presumably sourced in Belgium. However the Scanbus operation was relatively short-lived. When the route came up for retendering in 1989 it was won back by London Buses.

The pattern set in 1985 continued in 1986, with both Eastern National and London Country winning more services. Eastern National was gradually making inroads into the northeastern suburbs — Walthamstow, Loughton, Chingford — and adding Citybus fleetnames to those buses used on LT services. Initially these were Bristol VRTs; they were later joined by other types including Mercedes-Benz minibuses.

London Country picked up routes in a number of areas

London Transport may have been slow to react in the days before competition. But route tendering clearly changed things. Two low-cost London Buses operations successfully competed for tenders on opposite sides of London.

In Kent, the only sign that Orpington Buses was part of London Buses was the fleet numbering system applied to its 29 buses. The buses themselves were quite untypical of London Buses — Ivecos with Robin Hood bodies and stylish Optare CityPacers, all in a smart maroon and grey livery and carrying Roundabout fleetnames.

Orpington Buses was the smart approach. Stanwell Buses was the dowdy approach. This London Buses operation ran 28 vehicles — ageing Leyland Nationals — in LT red relieved by a half-hearted white and turquoise stripe. Stanwell Buses, serving Hounslow and Staines, traded as Westlink. It would later develop a more respectable image with a fleet which included Optare Deltas.

NBC subsidiary London Country was divided into four companies in 1986 in preparation for privatisation, these initially starting with prosaic geographical titles — London Country North East, London Country North West, London Country South East and London Country South West.

The deregulation of local bus services outside London, in October 1986, saw large numbers of redundant buses coming on to the secondhand market. It was a measure of the changes taking place in London that in 1985 LT was spending £250,000 on an Ogle design exercise for a new double-deck bus, while just two years later London Buses was snapping up secondhand Metrobuses and Ailsas from various Passenger Transport Executives.

Around this time LT was doing a brisk trade in selling Routemasters for operation in places where they either had quaint olde worlde charm or novelty value.

Opposite:
Harrow Buses took leased Metrobus IIs to commence its operations, one of which is seen in Harrow when new. These buses carried Birmingham registration marks, having been first registered by their manufacturer.

Opposite below:
Was humble pie on the canteen menu the day London Buses decided to buy back some of those unreliable Fleetlines from Clydeside Scottish? They were for the Bexleybus operation, as seen here in Woolwich.

Above:
Late delivery of new buses saw Maidstone Boro'line running a motley collection of hired vehicles. They don't come much more motley than this battle-scarred Atlantean from GM Buses, photographed in Bexley in 1988.

Left:
Boro'line's new buses for operation in Bexley were Olympians with Optare bodies to Leyland designs. One stands alongside a Hull Atlantean at Eltham station. The Atlantean, with Roe body (built in the factory which was later used by Optare), was covering for the late delivery of the Olympians.

43

A major buyer was Clydeside Scottish, and in a bizarre scenario which would not have been out of place in *Alice in Wonderland*, Clydeside was at the same time busy selling DMS-type Fleetlines back to London Buses.

The success of Stanwell Buses and Orpington Buses in 1986 saw two further local London Buses operations appear in the winter of 1987-8. The first, in November 1987, was Harrow Buses whose fleet included brand-new leased MCW Metrobus IIs, plus ex-West Midlands PTE Alexander-bodied Ailsas. Not all of the Metrobuses arrived in time, and for a period Harrow Buses was running ex-Greater Manchester Fleetlines, still in their original owner's brown, orange and white colours.

Manchester's livery, incidentally, could also be seen in Hounslow, where London Country SW was running an LRT service using ex-GM Atlanteans which it hadn't got round to repainting.

The second of London Buses' new operations was Bexleybus, which had a varied fleet including 28 new Northern Counties-bodied Leyland Olympians diverted from Greater Manchester where they would have been surplus to requirements. Other types operated by Bexleybus included the above-mentioned ex-Clydeside DMS Fleetlines, Leyland Nationals and MCW MetroRiders. Bexleybus started operations in January 1988 but was not without its problems which resulted in two of its routes being reallocated to another operator before the year was out.

That other operator was also one with a troubled future, but that wasn't apparent in 1987. Boro'line Maidstone was the catchy new name for Maidstone Borough Transport. It had a catchy new livery too, designed by Best Impressions.

Boro'line won four routes in the Bexley area, which started at the same time as the Bexleybus operation. For this it ordered 14 Olympians with Optare bodies — but, and you've heard this story already and you'll hear it again — some were late.

So Boro'line started off with some unusual buses including Hull Atlanteans and a Volvo Citybus demonstrator. When it took over two routes from Bexleybus in November it added such delights as an ex-Tayside Ailsa to its fleet. Vehicle availability took priority over standardisation. In the end Boro'line took only 11 of its shiny new Olympians, substituting the Volvo Citybus demonstrator and two dealer stock Scanias for the remaining three. Two of the Olympians later found use in London with Cityrama, for its second south London service in 1987.

More colour appeared in southeast London when London Country SE adopted a new name — Kentish Bus & Coach — and a new livery of cream and maroon to go with it. Kentish Bus, which was bought by the Newcastle-based Proudmutual group in 1988, expanded steadily by winning LRT tenders. Its biggest planned expansion came at the start of 1990 with the addition of 43 new Northern

Right:
Most of Grey-Green's new buses were mid-engined Volvos. These included East Lancs-bodied Volvo B10Ms for operation between Golders Green and Finsbury Park. One loads at Golders Green bus station.

Below right:
While most Routemasters in London have remained red, some variety was injected by Kentish Bus when it won the tender to operate the 19 using RMLs leased from LRT. This one is seen soon after entering service in 1993. In 1998 they were being repainted — red.

Counties-bodied Olympians to the fleet. Its biggest unplanned expansion followed in February 1992 when the overstretched Maidstone Boro'line operation was in the process of collapsing. Kentish Bus took over its London operations and 57 buses. This made Kentish Bus the largest private contractor to LRT.

Of more interest than new Olympians and Dennis Darts in the Kentish Bus fleet were the 24 Routemasters which it acquired to operate the 19 from Finsbury Park to Battersea Bridge. These, in full Kentish Bus livery, took to the streets in 1993. During 1998 they were being repainted red as Kentish Bus disappeared in a reorganisation of the London operations of the Arriva group which by then owned Kentish Bus — not to mention Grey-Green, South London, London & Country, County Bus & Coach, The Shires (formerly Luton & District) and Leaside Buses.

How Arriva came to own such a large chunk of London's buses is a story in itself. Let's just say it was the outcome of a long process of takeovers involving names which may have seemed important once but are fading from memory — Drawlane, British Bus, AJS, Cowie, Simco 314 (bet that one's stumped you) and Luton & District.

The distinctive new look adopted for Bexleybus (blue and cream) and Harrow Buses (red and cream, but in rather different proportions from those traditionally associated with London buses) rather overshadowed Kingston Buses which started in June 1987 but retained all-over red. The setting up of Kingston Buses was not the smoothest of operations.

The formation of low-cost operating units does, by implication, suggest that cost savings have to be made — and typically this affects staff wage rates and working conditions. Nobody likes a wage cut, and the Transport & General Workers Union decided to take London Buses to court in a challenge to the planned imposition of new working conditions. There were local stoppages in the Kingston area and a one-day strike which affected all but three London Buses depots before agreement was finally reached. Just as Kingston Buses remained in London red, so did Sutton Bus which took over much of the Sutton area network in 1988.

One new independent appeared on the list of successful tenderers in 1987 — Grey-Green Coaches — at that time the only transport company owned by the Cowie motor trade group. Grey-Green was an established coach operator, and its success in winning a tendered route in East London marked a significant change in direction. By the end of the year it had four routes and was running a mixture of vehicle types in a livery which was neither grey nor green. The buses included Leyland Lynxes, ex-South Yorkshire Metrobuses and ex-Manchester Fleetlines, soon to be joined by new double-deck Scanias. The livery was orange, white and brown — but that was to be short-lived.

In the autumn of 1988 a new livery which did include both grey and green — from the Best Impressions studio — was introduced on a fleet of 30 Volvo Citybuses when the company became the first independent to penetrate the heart of the capital. Grey-Green built up a varied bus fleet which included Ikarus-bodied DAF SB220s, Dennis Darts, Volvo Citybus single-deckers and nine bizarre Volvo B10Ms which had started life as coaches in 1985 but were rebodied as double-deck buses by East Lancs in 1992.

It could be argued that tendering really came of age in 1988 with two central London routes going to new operators in November. Grey-Green got the 24, which ran from Pimlico via Parliament Square and Trafalgar Square to Hampstead Heath. And Boro'line — its troubles still in the future — won the 188, which ran from Euston by way of Waterloo Bridge and various southeastern suburbs to

The LRT operations of Maidstone Boro'line were taken over by Kentish Bus in 1992. Until they were repainted, buses in Boro'line's attractive livery had Kentish Bus fleetnames added. This is a 1989 Alexander-bodied Volvo Citybus.

⊖ **BUS**

| 188 | GREENWICH (CUTTY SARK) |
| | ALDWYCH WATERLOO ELEPHANT |

PAU 196R  WILFRED

  ⊖ **BUS**

Greenwich. Late deliveries were a problem yet again, and Boro'line hired two-door 'deckers from Nottingham and Ipswich to cover the 188, pending delivery of new Alexander-bodied Citybuses.

So far, all LRT tenders had been won by local operators — NBC or ex-NBC subsidiaries around the fringes of the capital, independents based in the Greater London area, and municipally-owned Boro'line at Maidstone. That changed in September 1988 with the arrival of Frontrunner South East on the scene. This operation was set up by East Midland Motor Services, an NBC subsidiary which had been sold to its management earlier that year and had already established a toe-hold in Manchester where it operated under the Frontrunner name.

Frontrunner South East took over two services in the Romford and Gidea Park areas, with a fleet of 30 ex-Greater Manchester Atlanteans in East Midlands' attractive two-tone green and cream colours. Frontrunner South East didn't last long. East Midlands was bought by Stagecoach in April 1989, and in July the Frontrunner South East operation was sold to Ensign Bus.

Another new name in 1988 was Pan Atlas, which took over a route between Ealing and Palmers Green with eight Leyland Lynxes. These might have been outwardly similar, but were dealer stock vehicles to two different mechanical specifications. The service was taken over on 30 July — two days before the year prefix on registrations changed from E to F. Imagine the disbelief of the staff in the licensing office, up to their ears with documentation for the flood of F-registered cars taking to the road on 1 August, when someone asks to license eight vehicles two days before the E-prefix becomes last year's registration. Pan Atlas, which traded as Atlas Bus, expanded into double-deck operation in 1989 with another northwest London route. For this it bought nine Olympians with low-height Northern Counties bodies. Atlas Bus survived as an independent until 1994.

While the Bexleybus operation was set to go badly

wrong, it wasn't the only hiccup in 1988. A strike at London Country NE saw it lose three LRT tenders in February. Two were awarded to Grey-Green; the third went to Borehamwood Travel Services. This ran from Borehamwood to Edgware and among the vehicles used initially was a Duple-bodied Leyland Leopard in the livery of Thomas of Llangadog, a name which might have caused some comment in Edgware if anyone had known how to pronounce it. Borehamwood Travel Services soon started running ex-Yorkshire Woollen Atlanteans in a smart poppy red and yellow livery, using BTS as a fleetname, and followed these in 1989 with six new Alexander-bodied Scania 'deckers. Ultimately BTS would be best known, among enthusiasts at least, for its operation of Routemasters between Aldwych and Golders Green from 1993. BTS was bought by Blazefield in 1994 and its name changed to London Sovereign in 1996.

Yet another coach operator took an interest in running buses in 1989, with the arrival of R&I Coaches. It took over the operation of three services using new Iveco minibuses. Bigger expansion followed in 1990 with the arrival of a fleet of 14 Dennis Darts for a route taken over from London Northern — the company which would ultimately take over R&I in 1995.

The big name in small buses in the late 1980s was Transit Holdings, with minibus networks in Exeter and Oxford. In the spring of 1989 the company launched Docklands Transit which by the end of the year was running 70 Ford Transits with a target of 100. Docklands Transit was not operating under contract to LRT, but was instead running commercial services with LRT's approval. The company had five routes and ran for 18 months before closing down suddenly — giving less than three weeks notice — in November 1990. It argued that its exclusion from LRT's Travelcard schemes had undermined its viability.

Transit Holdings would reappear, this time as an LRT contractor, in 1993. It started running a few Mercedes and then graduated to routes requiring bigger buses — the

Opposite:
When Boro'line took over the 188 it suffered from the perennial LRT contractor's problem — late delivery of new buses. The odd buses hired in to provide short-term cover included this ex-Nottingham Atlantean which had been running for Ipswich. Lest anyone doubt that this apparition was a bus, those kind people at LRT have spelt it out above the destination display.

Left:
A shiny new Pan Atlas Lynx in Ealing on 30 July 1998 on its first day in service — even the wheels are still clean. It was one of eight. Pan Atlas disappeared in 1994.

ubiquitous Dennis Dart. It was taken over by Stagecoach in 1997 and absorbed into that group's East London operations.

By now LRT was not only issuing tenders for new routes, but the original contracts were expiring and were coming up for retender. In 1989 LRT claimed that around 25% of London's bus services involving some 1,500 buses had been put out to tender, and that London Buses had won around two-thirds of this.

A new name in 1990's tender awards was County Bus & Coach, part of the former London Country NE company whose operations had been sold in 1988 to the AJS group. County took over two former London Buses routes in Romford, for which it bought new Lynxes and Olympians. The Olympian route, the 103 from North Romford to Rainham, passed to Grey-Green after 18 months as part of a reorganisation of County Bus by AJS. (And that's where Simco 314 comes in — it ran the 103 for a short time after AJS had sold the bulk of County Bus to Lynton Travel.)

County had been set up in 1989, and at the same time the remainder of London Country NE was reformed as Sovereign Bus & Coach. Sovereign (owned by Yorkshire-based Blazefield Holdings from 1991) had some success in Harrow in the winter of 1990-1, and bought a fleet of new Mercedes minibuses for operation on routes which had previously been part of London Buses' Harrow Buses operation. This had faded away as much of the network had been lost to other operators when it was retendered, cutting its peak vehicle requirement from 110 to 34. Harrow Buses' new Metrobus IIs were returned to the leasing company and quickly found new owners elsewhere.

Bexleybus vanished too, after a little over two years, and its Olympians were also returned to the leasing company. The operation had had its problems and parts of it were retendered and won by other operators. London Buses argued, with some justification, that it wanted to capitalise on its instantly-recognisable red livery in an era

Above:

A sparkling BTS Routemaster pulls out of Golders Green bus station for the trip south to Aldwych. The operation now trades as London Sovereign.

Below

The changing face of London Leylands. On the left a preserved RTL, on the right a new Capital Citybus Olympian. The RTL is a 56-seater; the Olympian seats 77 in a body by Northern Counties. There were seven buses in this batch, all with 888 registrations. The number is considered by the Chinese to bring good fortune. The letters TTT on this bus are the initials of the company's then owner, T. T. Tsui.

when more and more differently coloured buses were appearing on the capital's streets. But it's hard not to conclude that the whole Bexleybus business was one which the powers that be thought might best be forgotten. Whatever the reason, the blue and cream livery soon disappeared.

Ensign Bus had expanded and by 1990 was running almost 90 buses. In the summer of that year it was announced that the company was being sold to an American buyer. This didn't happen, but at the end of the year it was sold to the owners of Hong Kong Citybus. This saw a change in identity, with the flag being lowered on the blue and silver Ensign Bus livery which gave way to yellow. The operation was renamed Capital Citybus. New vehicles being delivered at the time ownership changed were Dennis Dominators with Northern Counties bodies. Under Hong Kong ownership the company bought Olympians, a policy which continued after the company was the subject of a buy-out from its Hong Kong owners at the end of 1995 — but with the addition of Dennis Arrows too. In 1998 Capital Citybus was bought by FirstGroup.

On the other side of the capital Armchair, a respected coach operator which was running buses in a small way in Surrey, moved into London in the summer of 1990 when it took over the service between North Finchley and Shepherds Bush with a fleet of new Leyland Olympians with Alexander bodies. A second tender win saw these being joined by Leyland-bodied Olympians in 1991. Armchair's biggest expansion came in 1996 when it won work in the Ealing area which required a fleet of 25 Plaxton-bodied Dennis Darts.

Late deliveries of new buses for tendered routes could regularly guarantee even more colour on London's streets and at the end of 1990 it was London Country SW's turn. It was now trading as London & Country and had taken over the 188 from Oxford Circus to Penge, but its new Volvo Citybuses were not ready in time. This led to the strange sight of yellow and red Atlanteans from the Mainline fleet in Sheffield running through Trafalgar Square — not a location noted for the regular operation of Leyland's first-generation rear-engined double-decker since the trial of XA-class Atlanteans some 25 years earlier.

London Buses was undergoing change and in 1990 it was divided into 11 new bus-operating companies, plus London Coaches and the free-standing Stanwell Buses business. The biggest of the new bus companies was London General with 582 vehicles, while the smallest was Metroline with 343. This fragmentation of London Buses opened up competition for tenders between each of the new companies, and while generally such competition was at the borders of their existing operations some did flex their muscles and pursue tender opportunities remote from their existing territory.

One of the new companies, London Forest, only lasted a little over 12 months when it was closed following a

dispute between its management and workers about new conditions of employment. London Forest's work was shared between East London, Leaside Buses and London Central, while new tenders in Walthamstow — which had triggered the dispute — went to County Bus, Ensign Bus and Thamesway. The last-named had been

Top:
Armchair's first double-deckers were 12 Alexander-bodied Olympians in 1990. One heads through Ealing in the summer of 1997. The company also has Olympians with bodies by Leyland and Northern Counties.

Above:
Luton & District, Watford Bus and this green and grey livery have all disappeared since this photograph was taken in 1995 and the company was relaunched as The Shires — now in turn giving way to Arriva. A Leyland-bodied Olympian is seen in Watford. It is one of 15 delivered to London Country NW in 1989.

formed in 1990 to take over the London and south Essex operations of Eastern National which by that time was part of the Badgerline group.

London Country North West changed hands in 1990, being bought from its management by Luton & District. It was running LRT routes in the Harrow and Watford areas with new Darts and Olympians.

Two short-lived new names arrived in 1991. TGM Buses — the initials stood for Telling Golden Miller — was at that time a subsidiary of Midland Fox and won two routes in southwest London from Stanwell Buses, which TGM Buses operated with 13 Leyland Nationals. TGM — no relation to the post-1993 independent Telling Golden Miller operation which appeared on a tendered service in Sutton in 1995 — was quickly put under the control of London & Country, although its blue and white livery lingered on for a time.

Transcity took over a former Bexleybus minibus service, then in 1992 won a route requiring Darts in 1991, for which it purchased nine with Plaxton bodies. It sold out to Kentish Bus in 1993. London-based Thorpe took over operation of the Stationlink service in 1992, a route linking London's main line termini and designed to provide connections for disabled travellers. This started with Mercedes 709Ds, but in 1997 was upgraded to operation by Optare Excels.

Capital Coaches — not to be confused with Capital Citybus — branched into LRT bus operation in 1993, when it started running a service in the Hatton Cross area — a stone's throw from the company's Heathrow base. This used Mercedes minis; bigger buses followed in 1998.

In 1993 it became clear that the Government spoke with forked tongue — a surprise, perhaps, only to the naive. After insisting that London's bus services would be deregulated, it now insisted that they wouldn't — well, not yet, anyway. But the former London Buses companies would be privatised. First to go was London Coaches, sold to its management in 1992 and adding bus operation to its portfolio the following year, with 26 Titans for the 52. London Coaches bought Atlas Bus in 1994 and transferred route 52 to its new acquisition before selling it to Metroline. This all happened as Atlas Bus was losing its original two LRT routes. The Atlas name vanished in 1996.

The first example of a provincial operator winning an LRT tendered route had been East Midland, with its Frontrunner South East operation in 1988. And that hadn't lasted long. The next was a Liverpool-based company, Gemsam, which ran Liverbus. It won two LRT routes in 1993, for which it formed a new London Suburban business. This operated double-deckers from both ends of the quality spectrum — stylish new Volvo Olympians with Northern Counties Palatine II bodies, and tired old ex-London Buses Titans. And if Gemsam sounds an unlikely name for a company, it represents the initials of owners G. E. and S. A. Metcalf.

London Suburban lasted 18 months before being bought out by another Liverpool-based operation, MTL Trust Holdings. MTL had earlier bought London Northern as part of the London Buses privatisation programme.

At the start of 1995 British Bus reorganised its London & Country business, hiving off the London tendered operations to a new Londonlinks Buses company, which used a modified version of London & Country's two-tone green and red colour scheme. Control of Londonlinks moved to Invictaway in 1996 — an umbrella grouping of Kentish Bus and Maidstone & District. Then in 1997 Londonlinks slowly vanished, its operations being absorbed by other parts of the Cowie organisation. Thus some colour was lost as London red replaced Londonlinks green.

The pace of new arrivals then slowed down dramatically. Q Drive reappeared in 1996 with MetroRiders being operated between Victoria and the Elephant & Castle by its Limebourne Coaches fleet on a route won from London General. It added a Dart-operated route from Liverpool Street in 1997.

The next new name, Harris of Grays, expanded dramatically after winning its first tender in 1997. This was

run by Optare Excels, but Harris now also runs a growing fleet of eye-catching double-deckers on the eastern side of London, including Northern Counties Palatine IIs and East Lancs Pyoneers.

And a surprising new player appeared in 1998 — Travel West Midlands — taking over two former London General routes. This was in fact the company's second London foray. It had previously — before rearranging its name — owned the Westlink operation. West Midlands Travel, as it then was, had bought Westlink in 1994 (after the company had enjoyed 12 weeks of independence under a management buy-out) — and then resold it, to London United in 1995.

Now consolidation is the name of the game. Since privatisation in 1994, most of the 11 former London Buses bus-operating subsidiaries have become part of the major groups — Arriva, FirstGroup, Go-Ahead, MTL and Stagecoach — with only two, Metroline and London United, being non-aligned so to speak,

Add to this the fact that most of the independents have gone. MTL absorbed both R&I and London Suburban. In 1998 MTL's London business was in turn bought by Metroline. Cowie owned Grey-Green long before it had any thought of becoming a major player in the bus industry. London Buslines was bought by CentreWest, which is owned by FirstGroup, also represented in London by Thamesway.

Which leaves just Armchair, Harris Bus, Metrobus and Blazefield's Sovereign fleets as the big independent players. But they alone ensure colour and variety which was unimaginable in the early 1980s.

London Suburban, owned by Liverpool-based Gemsam, bought new Olympians and old Titans to operate its LRT tendered routes. An early Park Royal-built Titan — formerly T14 in the London fleet — is seen in Islington. After 18 months London Suburban was bought by MTL.

Londonlinks was a short-lived British Bus/Cowie operation which took over the London tendered services of London & Country at the start of 1995, and which was absorbed by other Cowie operations in 1997. An East Lancs-bodied Volvo carries the Londonlinks name on its previous operator's livery.

GOODBYE TO ALL THAT

As Arriva's corporate identity starts to take hold, PETER ROWLANDS celebrates the many popular liveries it is replacing, and reflects on the recent headlong rush to abandon individual colour schemes.

I've never seen an Arriva bus. One in the new corporate livery, I mean. As I write this, in the depths of January 1998, I have the sense that it's all a nightmare — that I'll wake up in five years' time and there'll still be blue and yellow buses in Luton, red and yellow ones in Derby, grey and red ones in Gosforth and two-tone green ones south of London. And so on.

Sadly, I fear this is no more than wishful thinking. By the time you read this there will probably be hundreds of buses in this livery all round the country, inexorably eliminating a wealth of former colour schemes.

The extent of change implied by this development is truly enormous. If you haven't fully grasped it yet you'd better prepare yourself now. All those Arriva (formerly Cowie group) fleets with their own distinctive liveries will disappear in the next couple of years. There will just be one Arriva identity wherever you go. Six thousand buses in over two dozen subsidiaries (that's ignoring London) will all end up looking the same.

Until this development, announced in October 1997, it was the Stagecoach group that took all the flak for imposing a rigid corporate identity on its bus fleets — or the credit, if you're in favour of it. But at least Stagecoach retained most of the names of its individual companies, which it reflected in a subscript to each fleetname.

Arriva is going much further down this road — not just adopting a single livery for all its subsidiaries outside London, but also doing away with individual fleetnames altogether. These are being replaced with a more generalised legend — 'through Kent and Sussex', for instance.

Top:
Northumbria's mould-breaking livery excited comment when it first appeared, but the bold blocks of colour made it one of the most distinctive in the country. An ECW-bodied Bristol VRT is seen in Newcastle.
ALL PHOTOGRAPHS BY THE AUTHOR

Above:
From the same designers came a bold new look for North Western which was modified in the early 1990s, initially using the red and blue in a simpler layout, and later adding yellow. The original layout is carried on a long-wheelbase Leyland Atlantean AN68/2 with Alexander body which had been new to Preston Borough Transport.

It's certainly a bold move; some would say an imaginative one. On the other hand if you regret the passing of the old liveries you'll be less enthusiastic. Whatever your feelings, you have to acknowledge there's never been anything like this in the history of British bus operation.

For those with any doubts, it must seem particularly ironical that by the time it made this total about-face, Arriva (or rather its Cowie predecessor) had become something of a standard-bearer for good taste and individual flair in bus liveries. In fact you could argue that in a subtle sense, Arriva already had a common identity of a kind. Although lacking outward resemblance to one another, its individual liveries increasingly shared a common flair for colour and shade, and an obvious respect for the proportions of the buses that bore them.

A notable feature was the way fleetname and livery began to be conceived together, so that they complemented one another rather than competing for attention. The significance of this kind of finesse seems to have been lost on groups such as FirstBus (now just First), which has imposed a standard fleetname style on a host of individual liveries.

Much of the credit for the more distinguished liveries at Cowie goes to a single design house, Best Impressions, whose Ray Stenning has single-handedly played a major role in defining the public face of the bus industry in the 1990s. His Cowie designs include Grey-

Green (where Cowie first came into the industry), Kentish Bus, London & Country, Maidstone & District and Luton-based The Shires.

However, Ray was not alone in bringing this new touch of class to the industry. Subsidiaries acquired late in Cowie's lifespan had often managed to create some striking new images for themselves before they joined the group. Perhaps the most notable was Northumbria, whose scheme of broad diagonal bands of grey and red with white trim always had terrific panache, and was maintained under British Bus (which Cowie bought in 1996). Another was North Western, which during the 1980s adopted a scheme from the same design team, with comparable diagonals. This was later much simplified on grounds of cost, but was then replaced by vibrant new livery of red, yellow and blue.

Indeed, if there was any obvious common element in the Cowie liveries in later years it was a drift towards schemes incorporating red and yellow in varying

proportions. Those colours had been adopted back in the 1980s by Clydeside and Midland Fox, and were later introduced at Bee Line, Derby City Transport (here again with blue), Midland Red North, Stevensons and Tees & District. The Shires' blue and yellow also had some reminiscences of these schemes.

However, the layout of these colours differed between fleets, as did the individual fleetnames; and the various implementations never came anywhere near to creating a national identity. That was yet to emerge.

What is doubly ironical about Arriva's conversion to uniformity is that until recent years its predecessors had looked fairly unlikely champions of good design. Cowie itself may have set a high standard with the crisp and clever Grey-Green (and orange) colour scheme. But other constituents had inherited a pretty motley selection of earlier liveries — some of them conjured into existence rather hurriedly in the 1980s, during or after their emergence in the privatisation of the National Bus Company. In many cases operators had been prevented from improving their liveries by lack of investment and cash-draining bus wars.

Perhaps most memorable (or forgettable) was the livery of the Bee Line low-cost unit in Manchester — never high in finesse, and in its early days often looking woefully neglected.

Yet against the expectations of many, the Cowie group came to grips with these issues and restored the image of its individual businesses. Fleet by fleet, old liveries were spruced up and new ones were invented. Even Bee Line became respectable. Arguably Cowie ended up with the best collection of individual bus liveries in the industry. And that's what we're now in the process of losing.

So is a single corporate livery valid? There are broadly two views about this. On one hand, running buses can be regarded very much as a business these days, where considerations of marketing and public identity should be paramount.

Above:

London & Country's two-tone green and red is an unlikely-sounding combination which actually worked very well. An East Lancs-bodied Volvo Citybus transferred to the Londonlinks fleet heads through Trafalgar Square in 1997, the year in which Londonlinks was wound up and its operations shared between other Cowie businesses in London.

Inset

Luton & District became The Shires in 1995 with an attractive new livery replacing two existing schemes — cream and red for the original Luton & District operation, and a sombre green and grey for the former London Country North West fleet. A Volvo B6 with Northern Counties body in Luton carries the Luton & Dunstable local identity as well as route-branding for a local service.

The argument here is that a single image becomes instantly recognisable, is easier to promote, and can become identified with a unified standard of service. It's worked for the high street retailers; why shouldn't it also work for buses? Seen in this light, separate liveries for a single group are illogical in a way. You wouldn't expect Boots to have a different design on every fascia, would you? So why should Arriva or Stagecoach take that approach to their buses?

Alongside this argument comes the one about operational benefits. A single livery allows operators to swap buses between fleets without having to repaint them. That can make it more flexible, quicker on its feet, and more ready to innovate and react to changing circumstances. It's a genuine benefit that can save thousands of pounds on every repaint avoided.

The other view of standardised liveries is that the vibrancy of local bus operation is best conveyed by a unique identity; that nationwide branding is irrelevant in a local context. Perhaps the most compelling argument on this side is that bus travel is local by definition. You don't expect to board a bus at one end of the country and arrive in it at the other. Even British Rail in its latter days recognised this logic, and adopted different liveries for trains on different regional operations. Local transport marketing became respectable.

Where there's a choice of local bus operator, presumably the concept of national branding has some merit. But in practice there seldom is a choice, even in this deregulated era. So the marketing argument, if there is one, is less about which operator you pick and more about whether you choose to travel by bus or not.

But will you be more comfortable about boarding a bus in an unfamiliar town if you recognise the operator from your home area? Perhaps; but personally I'm sceptical. When I'm in a strange town, if I'm wary of using its buses this is more likely to be through ignorance of the geography of the area, the locations of bus stops, the routes, the frequencies, the timings, the pricing regime and the routine for paying. Not to mention my anxiety about whether I'll recognise the destination when I get there. Address these issues first and worry about livery later (if at all) — that would be my advice.

On the question of the operational argument for a standard livery, you have to question who is actually gaining from it. The need for large-scale movement of buses between fleets is often a function of inter-operator competition, and that seldom has much to do with

customer benefit. In the short term it may lead to lower fares, but usually the eventual outcome is either a truce or the withdrawal (or demise) of one of the operators. Either way, the low fares seldom last long, and often the only winner is the victorious bus operator — complete with its standardised livery.

Perhaps the least admirable aspect of standardised liveries in the privatised bus operating environment is that in some ways they're not really aimed at customers at all. A prime objective sometimes appears to be to impress (or intimidate) fellow operators, and to catch the attention of existing or potential shareholders.

In either case, the livery is simply an implement in a great commercial game. Yet the sobering reality is that in pursuit of it, people in remote offices somewhere can make sweeping decisions that quite genuinely change the look of the landscape throughout the country.

Does all this sound unduly negative? Don't worry; the power and size of the big groups will ensure that you'll hear plenty in defence of standardisation in the next couple of years. The danger is that a message repeated often enough will eventually be believed.

The reality is that we don't need standardised liveries just because the big groups say so. To take an obvious and familiar analogy, we didn't need standardised beers in the 1970s, did we? It was convenient for the big brewers to persuade us we did, but large numbers of consumers united in opposition and the Campaign for Real Ale was born. As a result of it, an element of local character was preserved, even within the national brewing groups.

You could argue CAMRA was concerned with the actual content of the product, whereas bus liveries are superficial. So maybe we'll never see a Campaign for Real Bus Liveries. Perhaps that's a pity.

Certainly you don't have to look far for supporters of local liveries. You could probably include the majority of those who work at grass roots level in the bus business. Why else do individual companies within corporate groups so often and so proudly turn out show buses celebrating earlier colour schemes, or invent local liveries to designate routes with special branding?

Consider, too, the plethora of new liveries that emerged with the disbanding of NBC — implying a vast pent-up desire

Opposite above:

Grey-Green's attractive livery on an unusual East Lancs-bodied Scania K92 chassis. The K-series Scanias had an in-line engine; most Scania double-deckers were based on the transverse-engined N-series.

Opposite below:

A Plaxton-bodied Leyland Tiger in Darlington shows the final pre-Arriva United livery.

to assert local identity in defiance of the corporate monolith.

Or you could ask the customers and the community at large — people who might not write letters to their local papers in protest at the imposition of a corporate bus livery, but will nevertheless feel quietly aggrieved when a familiar part of their local townscape is abruptly removed forever. You must have met them; I have.

In the wake of Arriva's decision to adopt a standard livery, even the more open-minded enthusiasts are going to have to face up to a harsh reality. A lot of the visual diversity of the past bus industry is on the point of

disappearing. Traditionally, the appearance of buses has tended to be associated with their operating area; buses have become landmarks in their own right, almost like the architecture or the natural features of the place. Not any more.

While Cowie held back from this kind of standardisation, Stagecoach remained isolated in imposing a corporate style. Now, however, the floodgates seem to have been opened. FirstGroup (formerly FirstBus) has already decided that all its new buses are to have a single corporate livery, as well as

existing double-deckers with its special corporately-designed interior. Theoretically that will leave hundreds of older vehicles hanging on to former liveries for many years; but common sense suggests that the new scheme will actually spread faster than that.

Meanwhile, Go-Ahead has introduced a standard livery for all its fleets throughout the North East. Who is to say it won't extend this one day to the rest of its operations, which includes buses as far afield as Oxford and Brighton?

Although other substantial groups such as Travel West Midlands, MTL and Yorkshire Traction remain independent as I write this, some could easily end up being assimilated into the bigger groups, and taking on their corporate liveries. The true independents such as Wilts & Dorset or Trent could eventually go the same way.

There is a genuine prospect that in a few years' time, any bus you encounter anywhere across vast tracts of the country will bear one of just four or five nationwide colour schemes.

It may not come to this. Fashion always runs in phases. The years of NBC uniformity were followed by the explosion of new local identities in the 1980s. Something similar could happen again. But at the moment the writing seems to be on the wall (and not on Arriva's buses, if it's local fleetnames you're thinking of).

One of the paradoxes is that while liveries in the rest of the country are becoming standardised, London has retained its own red colour scheme, which is a formal prerequisite for operators tendering for central area business (even Arriva has had to toe the line here). Indeed, within London itself there is more variety in liveries now than for many years, since the individual operators all use their own variations on the standard theme.

However, possible changes in bus regulation are looming, and with them the prospect of other local authorities regaining more influence on their own bus operations. A return to some form of tendering is not inconceivable. Perhaps it's not unreasonable to speculate that some authorities might then follow London Transport's example, and demand local liveries for bus services in their area. The big groups bidding for the business would hate this, but many on the outside would raise a cheer.

In the meantime, the British bus industry seems destined to assume a relentless uniformity, the like of which no one could have guessed at 10 years ago.

It's a remarkable experiment — that's for sure. And arguably in a world where most buses look alike in terms of livery, it means more interest in future will be focused on the vehicles themselves. Unfortunately, though, with the bulk buying power of the big groups, diversity in vehicle design will tend to be diminished, too.

All the more reason, perhaps, to prize the dwindling group of municipal operators and independent groupings that retain their own liveries (and buying policies), and to suppress a sense of regret each time another of them sells out to a national group. Until fashion takes another radical shift, the vestiges of former variety seem set to

Opposite:
The use of yellow as a base colour became a feature of a number of British Bus fleets in the pre-Cowie era. One was Derby City Transport, which replaced its municipally inspired two-tone blue with a much more colourful livery. This is an Alexander-bodied Scania.

Above:
One of the last new liveries to be unveiled before the decision to go corporate was an attractive cream and green scheme for Maidstone & District, at the start of 1997. The colours recognised the company's heritage, as did the stylish retro-effect fleetname. The first new buses delivered in the scheme were Plaxton-bodied Dennis Dart SLFs.

become as valuable as they are increasingly rare.

Despite repeated attempts, until lately there has never really been a genuinely nationwide livery in the British bus industry. Tilling, the government-owned grouping after the war years, tried it by adopting two standardised liveries for the majority of its fleets — red and green. But the individual companies retained their own fleetnames, and there were often styling variations between fleets; and there was little in the way of special effort to market the virtues of their common ownership. So the individual fleets managed to preserve an air of mutual independence, despite any evidence to the contrary.

In any case, Tilling was by no means the predominant force in bus travel. It ran alongside the best part of a hundred municipal undertakings, all with their own fleet colours. And that's not to mention numerous independents and the privately-owned rival grouping British Electric Traction (which encompassed a far greater variety of colour schemes).

After 1968, when Tilling and BET were united under public ownership as the National Bus Company, the concept of having either red or green liveries was extended to the enlarged fleet, and there was now some real effort to promote the national image. The emerging presence of the double-N National symbol for the fleet helped. But the bus livery itself was unimaginative (and that's being charitable), having plainly been developed with cheapness as a prime consideration; and the impact of any nationwide promotion was muted to say the least.

When privatisation of NBC loomed in the early 1980s, the vestiges of this attempt at a nationwide image were soon thrown off. In its place, the individual companies all adopted their own separate fleet liveries, often reviving colour schemes abandoned years before.

So the new nationwide bus groupings of the late 1980s and early 1990s emerged into a world of almost unprecedented diversity of image, at least in modern times; and they have clearly regarded it as a challenge to come to grips with this.

Below right:
Midland Fox started switching from red and yellow to a distinctive dark blue shade, initially on its Urban Fox services in Leicester. A boxy East Lancs-bodied Scania is seen in the city centre.

Below:
Stevensons had traditionally used yellow, but as the company became more closely linked with Midland Red North, adopted a deeper shade with red relief — in effect the Midland Red North livery. A Leyland National 2 heads out of central Burton.

10 *100*

Two nice round numbers. Ten photographs from the camera of TIM CARTER of buses with 100 in their registration numbers.

Left:
Grayscroft Travel of Mablethorpe owned this 1981 Plaxton-bodied Leyland Leopard, although the Manchester registration gives a clue to its original owner, Yelloway of Rochdale. The location is Leicester.
ALL PHOTOGRAPHS BY THE AUTHOR

Below left:
Number 100 in the Southdown fleet was this Leyland National 1, seen in Worthing.

Below:
London Transport had four Routemasters with the registration number 100 — RM100 (VLT 100), RM1100 (100 CLT), RM2100 (ALM 100B) and this bus, RM1000 (100 BXL). It is seen at Showbus 97.

Above:
A 1984 Roe-bodied Leyland Olympian in the Yorkshire Rider fleet. Since it was delivered Roe has been supplanted by Optare, Olympian production now lies with Volvo, and Yorkshire Rider still exists, and buses in Bradford — where this one was based — are branded First Bradford.

Left:
A Micro Rider in the Yorkshire Rider fleet. This 1986 Ford Transit has a 16-seat Carlyle body. It is seen in Leeds. Buses this small soon vanished from most big operators' fleets — including Yorkshire Rider's.

Opposite above:
Bammant's of Fakenham with a broadly similar 1981 Plaxton Supreme to that owned by Grayscroft, but on a Bedford chassis and fitted with two-piece express doors.

Opposite below:
The ugliest of the 100s? Number 100 in the Ipswich Borough Transport fleet was a Dennis Falcon with East Lancs body. The square-cornered top windows sit uncomfortably above the main windows with their radiused corners — and as for that offset grille and badge…well, what can one say? This bus was called *Buzzard* — and the signwriter put that centrally below the windscreen — which seems strangely apt.

Above:
West Midlands Travel was the biggest user of the Leyland Lynx; 100 loads in Walsall.

Right:
The standard Mercedes-Benz front makes it difficult to identify some of the bus bodies fitted to the O.405 chassis. This bus in the Stevensons fleet was bodied by Wright of Ballymena. It was called the Cityranger.

Below:
Ensign Bus briefly sold the Yugoslavian-built FAP-FAMOS as the Ensign Charisma in the UK. It looked like a Mercedes-Benz O.303 — but cost a lot less. United Counties ran one.

BACK FROM THE BRINK

Bodybuilders in the 1990s

The UK's bus bodybuilders had some lean years in the late 1980s and early 1990s.
ALAN MILLAR charts the fortunes of those who survived.

B ritain's bus and coach bodybuilders are generally happier and a lot busier than they were 10 years ago. In many cases, they also are a very different bunch of people as an unprecedented number of old established names have dropped out of the market while relative newcomers have risen to prominence.

Things could have been worse. As industry commentators contemplated the end of the 1980s, there wasn't a lot to cheer up bodybuilders. Demand for big buses was falling at home, new low-cost converters were supplying the bulk of the new generation of minibuses being built in their place and mainland European competitors were taking a bigger slice of the coach market.

That decade saw the end of Leyland's Park Royal, Charles Roe and Eastern Coach Works subsidiaries, also Duple and Metro-Cammell Weymann. Willowbrook shrank

to a tiny rump of its former self, Marshall pulled out of bus building and Alexander, Northern Counties and East Lancs kept afloat by diversifying into minibuses and other products.

Then another recession bit deeply from the summer of 1990, more jobs were axed, receivers were called in at Northern Counties and Volvo closed Leyland's remaining

Above:
Duple was one of the casualties of the changes which hit bodybuilding in Britain. Its final coach body range comprised the related 320 and 340 — which broke from previous Duple practice in having only numbers, not names. A high-floor 340 on DAF SB chassis for London-based Angel Motors is seen on a wintry morning in 1987, prior to delivery. SJB

bodybuilding capacity at Workington. Those of us who care about such things could all too easily visualise ourselves filing past the catafalque on which the deceased remains of the country's last coach works might soon be placed for us to pay our final respects on the passing of another great British manufacturing skill like shipbuilding or motorcycle making.

Happily, we didn't need to. The market has recovered, Northern Counties was saved, Marshall has come back and newer players like Wright and Optare have taken the place of the fallen giants. Most depend for their future on satisfying the tough demands of large operating groups with immense purchasing power, while technological change — especially the arrival of lowfloor buses — has cemented much closer links with chassis makers.

Of the survivors of the old regime, few have experienced such dramatic change as Plaxton which, today, is a far larger and better balanced international business than at any time in its past. Its astonishing growth began in 1987 when David Matthews reversed his smaller Kirkby Central Group of coach, truck and car dealerships based in Anston, south of Sheffield, into older, Stock Exchange-listed Plaxton to create a new type of coach and bus supplier.

Plaxton was transformed overnight from being a rather old-fashioned coach bodybuilder into a business with potential to manufacture, finance, sell, part-exchange and support a range of coaches, buses and minibuses built at its main factory in Scarborough, at the Reeve Burgess minibus plant at Pilsley in Derbyshire (which the 'old'

Plaxton had bought in 1980) and by outside suppliers. Kirkby's car and truck dealerships provided further insulation from rapid shifts in coach sales.

Matthews, the ambitious son of a Yorkshire miner-turned-engineering contractor, also wanted Plaxton to stem the flow of imported coaches and compete against successful German, Belgian and Dutch manufacturers across mainland Europe, while breaking into the urban bus market at home and abroad.

This required huge changes. He wanted to improve build quality and increase production by keeping the Scarborough factory busy all year. Demarcation lines were broken and big fleet customers — like Shearings, Wallace Arnold, Park's of Hamilton and Excelsior of Bournemouth — were encouraged to have their next year's coaches built before the peak winter building months.

It invested in computer-aided design facilities and projects were put in hand to develop new European-standard coaches to replace the Paramount range launched in 1982 and to produce Plaxton's first-ever double and single-deck citybuses. At the same time, Matthews and his team were looking out for acquisition opportunities to shorten the development programmes and strengthen Plaxton's position in the market.

Leyland Bus, newly acquired by its management, was on the market in 1987. Northern Counties, owned by Greater Manchester PTE, was another possibility and when the Laird Group put MCW up for sale at the end of 1988, Plaxton gave very serious thought to buying the rights to the Metrobus double-decker and relaunching it in a joint venture with Iveco.

Left:
When Duple closed, production of its Dartline body was taken up by Carlyle, which had previously been a minibus builder. But Carlyle, too, would soon disappear from the bodybuilding scene. Thanet Bus operated this Carlyle-bodied Dart. SJB

Below:
One of the great success stories of the 1990s was the Plaxton Pointer, seen here on another 1990s success, the Dennis Dart. This is a low-floor SLF delivered to MTL in 1997 for its Wirral Peninsula operation and seen leaving the modern bus terminal at Woodside. SJB

Opposite:
Plaxton's best-selling coach body is the Premiere. An air-conditioned Premiere 320 is seen here operating as a commuter coach with Hutchison of Overtown. It is on a Volvo B10M chassis. SJB

None of these opportunities was pursued, but the involvement of Iveco — Fiat's truck and bus division — followed Plaxton's first tentative move into mainland Europe towards the end of 1988. In a potentially far-reaching deal, it bought Carrosserie Lorraine, Iveco's small-scale French coachbuilding subsidiary. Lorraine built about 100 bodies a year, all on Iveco chassis, and a new co-operation agreement committed Iveco to selling Lorraine coaches in France, while Reeve Burgess began bodying Iveco DailyBus chassis for the UK market. A small batch of Lorraine-bodied Iveco midicoaches was sold in Britain.

The idea was to expand at home and abroad with strong chassis manufacturers. Plaxton already bodied Volvo, Scania, DAF and Dennis coach chassis for the UK and saw Iveco and Mercedes-Benz as other key partners, especially in mainland Europe. In what was meant to begin something big, some Paramount-bodied right-hand-drive Mercedes-Benz O.303s were built at Scarborough in 1990.

The previous year had seen Plaxton expand in two directions, buying the rights to Duple's coach and rural bus range from Trinity, which wanted out of bodybuilding to invest in Dennis's expansion, and doubling in size by acquiring the Henlys car dealer chain from ADT. Henlys brought Rochdale-based minibus bodybuilder and converter Mellor into the fold, but the more significant long-term consequence of the deal was that Henlys' Chief Executive, Robert Wood, soon became Plaxton's Managing Director with Matthews as Chairman. A former General Manager of Volvo's UK truck operations, Scots-born Wood soon became identified as the strong man behind the enlarged group.

Matthews entered 1990 in pursuit of another acquisition opportunity. Alexander, the country's largest bus bodybuilder with factories in Falkirk and Belfast supplying UK and Far East customers, had been put up for sale

along with its Scottish parent company's other industrial interests and seemed a natural fit for Plaxton which, by then, was going cool on the plan for its own double-deck body.

Given the growth of the previous three years, it seemed almost a foregone conclusion that Matthews would succeed in this endeavour, yet his ambitions were thwarted when a management buy-in team got Alexander instead.

Despite this setback, which would have broadened Plaxton's customer base at a stroke, Matthews vision began to bear fruit in 1991. A new Plaxton single-deck citybus had been under development for some time and was to use an aluminium construction technique influenced by the Alusuisse system which was gathering a following in the UK and Europe. Although aimed initially at the home market, this was to be styled to appeal to mainland European operators.

Before it appeared, a smaller and ultimately more successful cousin was launched into a fast expanding new sector of the market. The Dennis Dart, unveiled in 1988, had begun life as a complete Hestair/Trinity product with a Duple body framed in the same Cromweld stainless steel as the 425 coach and styled by the same designer, John Worker. Plaxton had declined the opportunity to buy this body along with the rest of the Duple range, so the first few were built in Duple's fast-emptying Blackpool factory during 1989 before a somewhat unlikely buyer took over production.

This was Carlyle, the privatised Birmingham engineering works of the National Bus Company's Midland Red subsidiary. One of the more successful early minibus converters, it was following the trend into bigger coachbuilt minibuses and, correctly judged that the Dart would be the next step up. But Plaxton's misgivings about the Duple body were well-founded. Although it looked distinctive, features like bonded glazing and a windscreen that stuck

out farther than the front bumper made it costly to maintain, so Dennis quickly offered the Dart to other bodybuilders.

Plaxton's solution was to scale down and lighten the design of its new 12m single-decker, give it a more upright front to maximise interior accommodation and call it the Reeve Burgess Pointer. The Pilsley subsidiary had done well out of the switch to minibuses and, because Plaxton had produced very few big buses before that market plunged into freefall in 1985, Reeve Burgess's sales had all been incremental work. It was entirely logical that the Pointer would also be made there.

Except that Pilsley was bursting at the seams as its Beaver-bodied Mercedes and Renault minibuses were still in great demand. In what the world was told was just a temporary measure, the first Pointers were built at Scarborough where coach production had been hit badly by the recession. The Pointer got off to a flying start at its launch in early 1991 with an order from London Buses and it never looked back.

The big single-decker, christened Verde as part of David Matthews' campaign for buses to be seen as an environmentally green alternative to car commuting, followed a couple of months later. The first were on Scania N113 chassis with vertical transverse rear engines — an acquired taste in single-deck chassis layouts which only a few British operators have ever very happily acquired — and Scania ordered 15 for stock. A Dennis Lance followed later in the year and there was talk of offering the Verde on the Leyland Lynx underframe, only Volvo killed off the Lynx at the end of the year without letting bodybuilders near it. Its B10B successor wouldn't follow for several months.

With the double-decker shelved, the range update was completed in the autumn of 1991 with the Paramount coach's steel-framed successors, the Premiere and raked-

front Excalibur. A high-floor export version of Volvo's then new B12 rear-engined coach, christened Prestige, followed and was destined for test-marketing in France. Their radical new look was accompanied by the use of a new resin transfer moulding system to manufacture the skirt panels and front and rear ends.

Substantial fleet orders kicked off home market sales, but the Matthews dream was fast coming unstuck. Plaxton lost £1.15 million on its coachbuilding and sales in 1990 and, to preserve jobs and capacity at Scarborough, the profitable Reeve Burgess plant was closed soon after the Pointer was launched, with the Beaver joining its new Dart-based stablemate on the half-empty Yorkshire production

Above:
Reeve Burgess may have gone, but its spirit lives on in the Beaver 2, now built by Plaxton's small bus division at Anston, near Sheffield. The Shires took 14 Beaver 2s in 1997. While the original Beaver was available on a range of chassis, the Beaver 2 has been built exclusively on the Mercedes-Benz Vario. SJB

Opposite above:
Plaxton's Verde emulated modern European styling but found few buyers. The biggest order came from the Badgerline group on Dennis Lances. These included vehicles for Yorkshire Rider, seen here in FirstBus days in the guise of Leeds City Link. SJB

Opposite below:
Northern Counties' full-sized Paladin got off to a slow start but in the end outlasted Plaxton's Verde. Paladin buyers included Stagecoach, as seen here in Manchester. The chassis is Volvo's B10M. SJB

lines. All Reeve Burgess products were rebranded as Plaxton.

The Verde had ignited like a damp squib, with Scania only selling the bulk of its stock buses when Cardiff Bus needed new vehicles in a hurry after the collapse of National Welsh prompted it to take on extra routes. It wasn't until the end of the year that the first post-launch order was secured. Forty, on DAF SB220 chassis (a model to which it didn't have access for the home market), went to Dublin Bus in a never-to-be-repeated deal.

Worse than this, the coaches had been launched too soon. Tales of a seat collapsing on one of the exhibits at the Coach & Bus '91 show in Birmingham were a foretaste of big problems as the first deliveries went into the high profile fleets. The resin transfer moulding process didn't work well to start with and early coaches were also plagued with water leaks. Plaxton did its utmost to rectify the faults and incorporate design changes in the new models, but the experience shook the big fleets which placed their next few years' business with Van Hool and Jonckheere.

The City was becoming edgy and, having already seen several of his closest colleagues leave Plaxton during 1991, the year ended with Matthews' own resignation from the company, Robert Wood's elevation to Chief Executive and the subsequent renaming of the group as Henlys. By mid-1992, Mellor and limousine converter Coleman Milne were sold to their management, Lorraine (which ended up building a dozen Duple-designed 425s) was

closed and Scarborough streamlined production to build only on Volvo and Dennis big bus and coach chassis and Mercedes minibuses.

To add to Henlys' woes, the Cowie group, whose bus and coach interests were then confined to Grey-Green and the Hughes DAF dealership and rental operation, mounted a £30 million hostile takeover bid in May 1992. It wasn't clear whether Cowie really wanted the bodybuilding operations, but they became the focus of Henlys' vigorous and ultimately successful defence strategy.

In the midst of it all, Matthews (still Henlys' largest single shareholder) re-emerged to support Cowie's bid and announced that he was prepared to buy Plaxton back from the putative new owner and try and merge it with another

bus bodybuilder. He named no names, but Alexander's chief Ian Galloway sounded surprisingly receptive to the idea when invited to comment on Matthews' plans.

Henlys used the announcement of two large orders from Stagecoach and Badgerline — the latter including the first decent-sized batch of Verdes on the Dennis Lance — to fend off Cowie's bid. At last, the worst was behind Plaxton and Wood was able to view the future with more confidence as production was stepped up and sales of the Pointer, Beaver, Premiere and Excalibur began growing. Within three years, Reeve Burgess was reinvented in spirit, though not in name, when Beaver bus production was transferred from Scarborough to part of the Kirkby Coach & Bus site at Anston, and within four years Scarborough was bodying DAF coach chassis again.

Henlys was also able to realise another part of Matthews' vision for the group in May 1995 when it paid £10 million for Northern Counties and gained a firmer foothold in the big bus market. Northern Counties had been bought by Greater Manchester PTE — then its major customer — in 1983, but was floundering in the depressed market after deregulation and had been placed in administrative receivership in 1991.

The outlook for the Wigan-based company looked bad until Volvo's closure of the Leyland bus plant in Workington and withdrawal from UK bodybuilding provided a lifeline for its rivals. Northern Counties' management developed new double- and single-deck bodies and bought the company in August 1992.

After Henlys took over, the ranges were streamlined and the surviving Northern Counties products — all, conveniently, with 'P' model names — were rebranded as Plaxton within a couple of years. The Palatine double-deckers — built mainly on Volvo Olympian, but also on DAF and Dennis chassis — had no Plaxton counterparts and took the group into a market it had long wished to occupy.

The single-decker ranges overlapped, with both plants producing their own designs for the Dart and its less successful Volvo B6 competitor. Both also produced 12m bodies — the Northern Counties Paladin on Scania L113, Volvo B10B, DAF SB220 and Dennis Lance; the Verde mainly on Lance, but also a few B10Bs. A prototype lowfloor Paladin, on the SB220, was under development at the time of the takeover.

The streamlining resulted in the Pointer, available in lowfloor form from October 1995 and even more successful then, becoming the only Dart and B6 body, while the big Paladin replaced the Verde as outstanding orders were either fulfilled or transferred to Wigan. The lowfloor Paladin — renamed Prestige in 1997 as the B12 coach had flopped in Europe — became the standard 12m lowfloor.

Prestige production was transferred from Wigan to Scarborough, leaving the Northern Counties factory to produce only double-deckers for home and Far East customers.

At the same time as Northern Counties was acquired, Henlys also expanded abroad in a big way — but in North America rather than Europe. In a joint venture with Volvo, Henlys bought a 49% stake in Prevost Car — one of the leading manufacturers of coaches on the other side of the Atlantic with 25% of the market — from the Quebec government. Volvo, hoping to wean American and Canadian operators on to its own engines and drivelines, bought the other 51% with the whole deal going through for £65 million.

With output of over 900 coaches a year, Prevost is a far more formidable business than Carrosserie Lorraine could ever have been, but it became even larger at the end of 1997 when its new owners paid £21 million for transit bus manufacturer NovaBUS. Owned latterly by Canadian rail manufacturer Bombardier (which built buses in Ireland in the early 1980s) and the Dial Corporation (the old Greyhound coach group), NovaBUS had inherited General Motors' North American bus manufacturing interests. It built GM's designs and a new lowfloor model at three factories in the United States and Canada, with a combined output of over 1,300 vehicles and a third of the market.

Before it added NovaBUS, more than 80% of Henlys' profits came from its bus and coach operations and it took them to 100% during 1997 by selling the tightly-squeezed car retailing side for over £50 million — a move unthinkable only six years earlier when buses and coaches were the weak link. The group changed name again — back to Plaxton — and was able to fund its share of the NovaBUS purchase from the proceeds of the sale of the car dealerships.

At home, Plaxton's product ranges were further expanded. The Cheetah coach body was developed to replace the luxury Beaver built at Scarborough. And a prototype President lowfloor double-decker was produced at Wigan ready to capitalise on a new trend in vehicle operation.

The developments at Northern Counties were paralleled by change at Alexander. Its new owners forged close trading links with Stagecoach as it began placing large orders to renew its fast-expanding fleet. Contracts for double-deckers were also won from Dublin Bus, while valuable export business continued to be secured in Hong Kong and Singapore.

A much-needed updating of the product range was begun. The PS-type single-decker was joined in 1991/2 by the Strider on rear-engined Volvo, Dennis and Scania chassis and by the Dash midi on the Dart and B6, while the R-type double-decker, first launched in 1980, was given a make-over in 1993 as the Royale. The Belfast plant developed the Setanta citybus for the Irish Republic, with initial deliveries on DAF SB220 chassis.

By far the largest proportion of production at both plants was on Volvo chassis, but Alexander also tried to work with the same ambitious pan-European giants as Plaxton had identified in the late-1980s. In 1991/2, prototype TurboCity

double and single-deckers were built for Iveco and two Mercedes-Benz O.405s were bodied — a rigid demonstrator and an articulated version for Grampian. Iveco's plans got nowhere and Mercedes pursued O.405 sales with other bodybuilders. Other diversification included making the bodies for driverless people-carriers at British and American airports — including London Stansted.

It soon became clear, though, that this was another management-owned company that needed a bigger owner's resources for its longer term survival and, in mid-1995, it accepted a £26.4 million offer from Mayflower, a Stock Exchange-listed British-owned automotive engineering group.

In the immediate aftermath of the takeover, Mayflower became excited by the prospects in the Far East, especially mainland China as Hong Kong was being returned to Chinese rule. But as some of the region's economies began overheating in 1997, more emphasis went back on to the home market where some long-established customers had switched orders to rival suppliers.

Stagecoach, Dublin Bus and Lothian continued to be Alexander's biggest British Isles customers, but double-deck orders were secured from FirstGroup while Arriva (the renamed Cowie group) ordered DAF double and single-deckers.

Mayflower completely replaced the product range in 1996/7. The Sprint minibus, developed from a product launched immediately after deregulation, was restyled (twice) as the ALX100, while new lowfloor products were introduced: the ALX200 on the Dart and B6; ALX300 on 12m single-deckers; ALX400 on two-axle double-deckers; and ALX500 on six-wheel export double-deckers.

All retained the welded aluminium structure long used by Alexander, setting them apart from the Ultra, a blind alley that Volvo had led the former owners into in 1994.

When lowfloor single-deckers started to take off in the late-1980s, Volvo put a lot of commendable effort into finding an ideal layout of vehicle. It recognised that wheel dimensions determine how many seats can be accommodated and produced a running prototype with six small wheels and twin-steering — a reinvention of the somewhat discredited Bedford VAL coach and one of the early ideas for the Leyland National.

Hardly surprisingly, when these thoughts were turned into the B10L — a pan-European lowfloor citybus capable of having up to three doors in left-hand-drive versions — the wheel dimensions were more conventional and there were just two axles. But Volvo also owned Säffle Karosseri, a Swedish bodybuilder which had developed its own bolted aluminium structural system called System 2000 —

technology which provided the strength needed on lowfloor buses.

As Volvo was keen to sell complete B10Ls across Europe, the close working relationship that already existed between the two companies made Alexander an obvious partner to build the Säffle body in the UK. A licensing agreement was signed to build the Ultra exclusively on the B10L, but there also was talk of System 2000 later being introduced across the Alexander range.

Ulsterbus and Citybus ordered 90 Ultras and production began at the Belfast plant. Timeline of Wigan and Dublin Bus also bought some, while a handful of gas-fuelled versions went to Travel West Midlands and Northampton Transport, but the Ultra hardly took the market by storm as customer pressure compelled Volvo to allow B10Ls to be bodied by Wright in rather more respectable quantities.

Wright, indeed, has been one of the phenomena of the 1990s. Formed in 1946 as a two-man family-owned commercial vehicle bodybuilder in the County Antrim town of Ballymena, it was virtually unknown on the British mainland for its first 30 years, even though that period saw it grow steadily into a specialist manufacturer in Northern Ireland. It built mobile libraries and shops, rural school buses, even a couple of two-door Ford R1114s for Sureline of Lurgan in 1973, but it wasn't until the early 1980s — after it became the first UK company licensed by Alusuisse to use its bolted aluminium structural system — that Wright began to break into the mainland PSV market.

It would take the best part of 10 years for operators to recognise the opportunity that Alusuisse creates for buses to be made much stronger and to consistently high standards, as well as making them quicker and easier to repair than traditional welded structures. These advantages were complemented by fast repair techniques for body panels.

Maidstone Borough was Wright's first major mainland conquest, with eight Bedfords supplied in 1982, and the

stylish Contour coach — developed in close co-operation with Bedford — followed soon after. But mainland penetration remained minimal until 1990 when London Buses ordered 90 NimBus bodies on Renault S75 minibus chassis. This was a turning point, as Wright was moving into new premises and soon concentrated exclusively on PSV buses, the vast majority of them for customers outside Northern Ireland.

The initial London order was followed by sizeable batches of Handybus bodies — a design that looked straight out of a 1950s catalogue, but was exceptionally practical on the Dart. It also won early favour with the Go Ahead Group. A steady stream of new designs soon followed from Ballymena, where talented Ford-trained Design Director Trevor Erskine's flair was translated into some increasingly stylish and innovative products, starting with express coaches on Ulsterbus Leyland Tigers and the first 12m urban buses — Endurance bodies on Scania K93s for Yorkshire Traction — in 1991.

Valuable future business was secured at this point when the then relatively small GRT Group switched body orders on Scania N113s and Mercedes O.405s for its Grampian and Midland Bluebird fleets from Alexander to Wright, and close working links were forged with Volvo as it launched the B10B in 1993.

All this was a prelude to the moment it became clear that Wright was aiming for centre stage. William Wright, Chief Executive and co-founder of the company along with his father, kept himself abreast of international developments by visiting European exhibitions. By the time he was making these visits in the late-1980s, he became impressed by the pace with which the German bus industry was re-equipping itself with lowfloor buses.

While others could see the benefits lowfloor would bring for wheelchair users and people with less disabling mobility problems, yet found it hard to imagine how cash-strapped British operators would ever fund the extra cost of buying them, William Wright was among those who judged that this was an irresistible trend. The disability lobby was one that politicians seldom dared ignore and, for an ambitious small-volume bodybuilder looking for a unique selling proposition, getting in at the start of lowfloor operation was an astute short-cut to growth.

The first Wright Pathfinder lowfloor was unveiled in 1993. Beneath the skin, it benefited from the inherent strength of Alusuisse, as lowfloor bodies bear many stresses carried on the more substantial chassis frames of higher floor vehicles.

London Transport generated serious British interest in lowfloor buses by announcing plans for a 68-vehicle, five-route trial. While competitors looked on, Wright's scooped the complete order on 30 Scanias based on a low front/high back compromise chassis launched first in Scandinavia, and on 38 British-built lowfloor Dennis Lances. A small batch of Lances followed for a Department

of Transport-sponsored trial with Go Ahead on Tyneside and as these led to other locally-funded projects, Wright was well placed to capture a good share of the orders.

A steady stream of similar-looking, if differently-named — try Crusader, Liberator, Renown, Axcess-ultralow and Axcess Floline for size — bodies followed on Dart, Volvo B6, B10L and B10BLE, Scania L113 and L94 over the next four years. In 1997, Wright got ahead of its competitors again with the Floline ramped floor system which virtually eliminates the height difference between the front and rear sections, and also allows 12m lowfloor bodies to have gasket glazing rather than bonded glass which is slower and more expensive to repair.

More was being promised as William Wright was tantalising the industry with the promise of a Millennium bus before the end of 1999.

Below:

Wright were leaders in the move to accessible buses, winning an order for 68 Pathfinder bodies for operation in London. Leaside Buses was among the early users, specifying Scania chassis. Alan Millar

Opposite above:

Optare's two best-known small buses. On the right, the eye-catching CityPacer, based on MAN-VW running units. The more successful MetroRider integral passes on the left. The operator is Cambus. Alan Millar

Opposite below:

One of Optare's strong points has been styling flair, a feature which is watered down on the Prisma which uses the standard Mercedes-Benz front-end structure which is neat enough, but lacks the impact of, say, the Delta or Excel. A Tees & District Prisma arrives in Darlington. SJB

This pace of product development was paralleled by several major extensions to the Ballymena factory and some impressive penetration of the market, with substantial repeat orders placed by Travel West Midlands and — thanks to that early order from GRT — from FirstGroup which made Wright its main supplier of 12m single-deckers from 1996 with articulated models to follow for 1998/9.

Optare has been the other major phenomenon of the 1990s. It arose out of the ashes of Charles Roe in 1985, taking over the Leeds factory and building some of its old designs as it sought work from anyone prepared to show faith in redundant craftsmen who believed there was life beyond Leyland.

Had it carried on in that vein, Optare might well have gone the way of countless other optimistic employee buyouts, and been overwhelmed either by the traumas of deregulation or the 1990/1 recession. But it was blessed by being led by a visionary Managing Director in Russell Richardson, a former Leyland and Duple man who was unafraid to be different and develop products even his customers didn't realise that they might want to buy. And by starting from scratch without any of the demarcation traditions that hindered competitors, he ensured that this operation could adapt quickly and focus on quality.

From the launch of the CityPacer minibus in 1986, he established a reputation for Optare as a manufacturer of well-built, eye-catching, practical and competitively priced products, that were different from anything coming out of rival manufacturers' factories and which were in tune with the operating needs of the day. It was an approach that made people think very quickly of Optare and know what it stood for without also needing to remind themselves: 'Oh yes, they're the people who used to be Charles Roe.'

To be fair, this wasn't always an unqualified success. Some products — and the CityPacer was one of them —

enjoyed more hype than sustained sales, but Optare always managed to have another model ready to offer a unique solution to an emerging trend.

In 1989, it helped secure its longer term survival when it bought the rights to MCW's bus designs from the Laird Group and rapidly relaunched the Metrorider integral mini/midibus as the MetroRider with a big 'R' in the middle. The first purpose-designed mini, rather than a van-based product, the Metrorider had been an overnight sensation from its launch in October 1986, with over 1,000 sold in the first two years.

But it sold below its true cost and quality problems sullied its reputation. Optare cured the major weaknesses before resuming production and concentrated on profits rather than

production volumes. Both strategies worked, but the purchase of the MCW designs also turned Optare from being a bodybuilder into a complete vehicle manufacturer, giving it more control over its destiny and also enabling it to earn useful profits from supplying parts and service to the large parc of MCW Metroriders, as well as the growing fleet of its own MetroRiders.

Right from the start, Optare preferred its dealings with chassis manufacturers to be on a firmer basis than had been the norm for coachbuilders before the mid-1980s. Instead of bodying virtually any chassis its customers chose to buy, it developed complete products with unique features and supported them with a comprehensive aftersales programme provided jointly by its own and the chassis builders' resources.

This was how the CityPacer was developed exclusively with Volkswagen and the larger StarRider with Mercedes. In 1988, the same approach was taken when Optare teamed up with DAF to challenge Leyland's integral Lynx in the steadily growing 12m single-decker market. Optare followed Wright's example and secured Alusuisse licensing for a mould-breaking streamlined bolted aluminium body christened Delta, while DAF brought its recently-launched SB220 chassis into the UK for the first time.

The Delta triumphed where the Plaxton Verde/Scania N113 would struggle two years later, selling partly to customers like Blackpool Transport which had graduated from the CityPacer. And even though the SB220 was later offered in the UK with Hungarian-built Ikarus and Northern Counties bodies, it's some measure of Optare's success that the Delta name was better known for a long time than the DAF's model number. Such is the power of Russell Richardson's marketing skills.

Optare followed the Delta in 1991 with the smaller and less immediately successful Vecta based on MAN's 11.180 large midi, but the link with DAF continued as the Dutch firm was developing the DB250 double-deck chassis from MCW's Metrobus. Optare and Alusuisse created the Spectra body — another ground-breaking design which prompted Northern Counties and Alexander to revamp their double-deckers within months of the Spectra's debut in October 1991.

The link with DAF was deeper by then. As it struggled to survive in the international truck market, DAF discarded some non-core activities and in 1989 hived off its bus division to United Bus, a new company which, despite its English name, was also Dutch and indeed was part-owned by DAF. United Bus also bought Bova, one of the Dutch coach manufacturers that had made life tougher for Duple, Plaxton, Leyland, Bedford and Ford in the UK and was in the market for other acquisitions beyond the Netherlands.

Optare was an ideal fit. It was acquired in 1990, gaining United Bus's sales resources to dip its toe into mainland European markets, selling Spectras to Turkey and also becoming the hub of DAF and Bova's UK operations. There also were plans to use the group's resources to seize niche market opportunities at relatively short notice; had these plans come to anything, London Transport's 68 pioneering lowfloor buses might have been Optare-badged right-hand-drive versions of Dutch or Danish citybuses.

But events got in the way. DAF itself went bust at the beginning of 1993 and although it was rescued in many bits, United Bus followed it into collapse before the end of the year. A sharp drop in the Dutch bus market, felt most acutely at the Den Oudsten subsidiary, had pushed it over the edge.

Again, many of the constituent parts were rescued and Optare, happily, was among them with Russell Richardson leading another management buyout to return the business to independence. Interest from Cowie, whose Hughes DAF subsidiary was sole DAF Bus dealer for the UK, apparently drove up the price. DAF Bus became part of the Dutch-owned VDL engineering group and made Hughes DAF its UK importer, so Optare's links with its former owner became significantly looser, even if it continued bodying both the SB220 and the DB250 and in 1997 unveiled Britain's first lowfloor double-decker on a redesigned DB250.

In the short term, Optare filled some of the gap by adapting the Delta/Vecta body to fit the Dennis Lance chassis and calling this model Sigma, but Dennis' policy of offering its chassis to as many bodybuilders as possible meant this wasn't an exclusive product. It was followed in 1995 by the Prisma, the latest in the rapid succession of bodies offered on Mercedes' O.405.

Structurally, the Prisma was another chip off the Delta block, but Mercedes' insistence on fitting its own front end — as it had also done with Alexander and Wright — robbed it of much of Optare's distinctive styling. The step-entrance Prisma was launched well into the lowfloor revolution and was obsolescent if not obsolete from the start, but Optare's marketing skills achieved more than Mercedes had ever done in nearly 30 years of trying to persuade British operators to buy its large buses and coaches.

Initial sales were helped by GRT switching its O.405 body orders from Wright, but Optare milked its potential to the maximum with orders pulled in from North East Bus and East Yorkshire as well as several smaller operators looking for a well packaged full-size bus. Mercedes had never done so well.

But helpful as these short-term measures were in getting Optare back in business — and in overcoming an understandable downturn in DAF sales — they hardly displayed the company's legendary flair and innovation. Those qualities came back to the fore in October 1995 with the launch of the integral Excel, Optare's first lowfloor product.

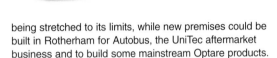

By then, the main chassis manufacturers all had established links with bodybuilders to offer lowfloor single-deckers: Volvo with Wright, Plaxton/Northern Counties and Alexander; Scania with Wright; DAF with Plaxton/Northern Counties; and Dennis — whose Dart SLF was about to prove even more successful than its step-entrance predecessor — with just about everybody. The Excel offered something different in the Dart's sector of the market.

To over-simplify matters, it is a big MetroRider, using the same steel structural technique and even its Cummins B-Series engine, but in front entrance/rear-engine format. While British bodybuilders prefer to make aluminium-framed buses, steel is cheaper and more widely used in other markets. Aluminium is lighter and more corrosion resistant, but Optare follows Continental practice by using sophisticated protection systems. It also argued — rightly or wrongly — that many operators were more interested in initial purchase price than long-term ownership costs.

Apart from giving the Excel a dramatically different look, with a very large windscreen, Optare also offered an 11.4m version — longer than any Dart available at the time. It's some measure of the Excel's impact that, although sold in smaller volumes than its Dennis rival, it nonetheless appeared to have prompted Dennis to team up with Plaxton to develop the 11.3m semi-integral Super Pointer Dart during 1997.

By then, Optare had followed the Excel with the rear-engined, Mercedes-powered Solo, the first really practical lowfloor mini/midibus and an eventual successor to the MetroRider. Coupled with contracts to export various MetroRider-derived vehicles to Malaysia, Sri Lanka and Australia, Optare was rapidly diminishing the importance of its aluminium body-on-chassis work.

It also expanded during 1996 by acquiring Autobus Classique, one of the more successful new businesses to have grown out of the upsurge in demand for light truck-derived midicoaches in the 1980s. It had been through the mill, as its founders set up the Rotherham business after another converter and bodybuilder — Europa of Doncaster — went into receivership, but was establishing a following at the upper end of the market.

For Optare, which dropped the cumbersome Classique name, Autobus offered several advantages: it re-established itself in a market sector last served with the StarRider coach; it gave it another arm to its business; and it provided room for expansion. The Leeds factory was

being stretched to its limits, while new premises could be built in Rotherham for Autobus, the UniTec aftermarket business and to build some mainstream Optare products.

While Optare, Wright, Alexander and Plaxton went on steadily upward growth curves, there was more of a rollercoaster ride for East Lancs, Marshall and Wadham Stringer/UVG.

East Lancs, 50 years a bus builder with a customer base centred on smaller municipal fleets, changed hands in 1988. For the previous 25 years, it had been part of John Brown Engineering but was among peripheral activities — Craven Tasker trailers was another — sold off by JBE's then owner, construction giant Trafalgar House.

There could hardly have been a worse time to sell. The market overall was depressed, municipals were on the brink of virtual extinction and East Lancs lacked credibility

Opposite:
For the Dennis Dart SLF Wright introduced the low-floor Crusader body, seen here in operation with CMT in Liverpool. MTL has also bought large numbers of Wright bodies on Scania and Volvo chassis, one of which is seen in the background. Alan Millar

Above:
Rebuilding and rebodying kept East Lancs busy during the most difficult years in the late 1980s and early 1990s. Its Greenway reworking of the Leyland National was bought by a number of operators including the local Blackburn Borough Transport fleet. Many Greenways were re-registered in an attempt to hide their real age. This one retains its original registration, which reveals that it was a former London Buses National 2. SJB

with other potential customers. But salvation came in the unexpected shape of emerging privatised bus giant Drawlane.

Maybe sentiment played a part, as former municipal manager Geoffrey Hilditch was then a senior director on its board, but the public version of events was that it wanted to protect bodybuilding capacity. If East Lancs disappeared, it might find it harder to obtain the numbers of affordable new buses it knew it would need before long. So East Lancs made up for the loss of disappearing municipal business by supplying fleets like Midland Red, North Western and London & Country which would never have considered buying from it before.

Not that Drawlane was the most consistent large scale purchaser of new buses. Indeed, its fleet was ageing faster than it was being replaced. But this helped push other work into the Blackburn factory. Leyland Tiger coaches were rebodied as buses and valuable revenue was generated within the group and for outside companies by heavily refurbishing Leyland Nationals as Greenways from 1991 onwards. More conventional rebodying work was also won, partly because few other companies were prepared to do it — especially after the last remnants of Willowbrook closed down.

Further change came at the end of 1992 when Drawlane hived off its bus operations to British Bus and East Lancs became part of a separate, but related business. A new factory was opened two years later with scope for substantial increases in production and, by 1995, British Bus had abandoned Leyland National refurbishment and was back buying new bodies from East Lancs.

John Worker, who also helped develop Alexander's ALX range, was called in to produce a new family of products — the Cityzen and Pyoneer double-deckers (Pyoneer started as Premyer until Plaxton objected) and Flyte and Spryte single-deckers. And it adopted the Alusuisse system which helped it improve build quality.

As well as bodying Scania, Volvo and Dennis chassis — the Scania relationship had been developed throughout the 1980s — East Lancs added MAN in 1997 and was prepared to take on work others might flinch at even considering. A couple of American-built Spartans were bodied for regular customer Yorkshire Traction in 1995/96 at a time when British Bus was also looking fairly seriously at the Spartan and it later tried to develop export business with the Americans. A one-off lowfloor chassis, called the Kirn and developed by people associated with the Ward and ACE companies in the 1980s, was also to be bodied for Yorkshire Traction.

But just as these advances were being made, British Bus was sold to the Cowie group which instantly severed its links with East Lancs. So instantly, in fact, that some outstanding orders were either cancelled or diverted to Plaxton and a space opened up in the Blackburn order books.

In the short term at least, much of it could be filled as demand for double-deckers — especially the immediately available ones that contractors need for London Transport routes — was exceeding other companies' ability to supply and Pyoneer orders were pulled in from a whole new

bunch of customers. By the end of 1997, even more unusual business was won in the shape of open-top left-hand-drive Pyoneer-bodied Volvo B10Ms for tour bus operator Guide Friday to run in Paris and an assembly contract had been secured to build Duple Metsec kit bodies for Hong Kong.

There still were clouds on the horizon, some blown over after the company's owner, former British Bus Chairman Dawson Williams, was jailed for corruption offences. But if it had to be sold again, there was a lot more for competitors or outside investors to buy than if East Lancs had been offered for sale five or 10 years before.

Marshall's return to the market came just as the industry began its slow climb out of the depths of recession in 1991, around the same time as, on one hand, David Matthews was leaving Plaxton while, on the other, Stagecoach had just placed one of its first major orders with Alexander.

Unlike most of its competitors, Marshall didn't depend on buses to survive. It was primarily a car and commercial vehicle dealer and an aircraft refurbishment specialist which had shown great foresight in developing Cambridge's airport in 1929 — a valuable piece of real estate that helped keep it independent of larger groups. Much of its aircraft work was military, so here was a business which enjoyed a good World War 2, a good Cold War and a good Falklands War, but it also needed useful civilian activities to tide it through the nation's less belligerent years.

As far back as 1946, it found work for under-employed aircraft tradesmen by setting up a commercial vehicle bodybuilding division which won a London Transport contract to refurbish prewar bus bodies. But new bus bodybuilding had to wait until July 1959 when an opportunity arose to buy Mulliner, the Birmingham-based military and export specialist from Standard-Triumph, and transfer production to a spare hangar in Cambridge.

That venture grew through the 1960s, began to wane in the 1970s after prime customer BET was absorbed into the National Bus Company, and closed in 1985 as the mainstream bus market went into meltdown.

While closure made sense in 1985, the end of the Cold War compelled defence contractors like Marshall — and the vastly bigger GEC — to find more civilian work. The remnants of the commercial vehicle bodybuilding operation became a new Special Purpose Vehicles division around 1989 and niche market products were added mainly as other businesses went into liquidation.

To go along with car transporters, Shelvoke dustcarts and Bedford trucks, Marshall seized its chance to get back into buses when the Carlyle Group went into liquidation on the eve of the Coach & Bus '91 show. Carlyle's parts and dealership businesses went elsewhere, but 33 years after the Mulliner purchase, Marshall was confident it could once again make a go of transferring a Midlands bus bodybuilder to Cambridge.

Carlyle had been overtaken by Plaxton, Wright, Alexander and Northern Counties in the Dennis Dart market, but had just begun transplanting its Cromweld stainless steel technology into coachbuilt minibus bodies when the business collapsed. Indeed, a Cromweld-framed body was still exhibited on an Iveco chassis at the 1991 show, offering the durability of aluminium at lower cost.

Coachbuilt minibuses provided the bedrock for the bus operation at Cambridge while urgent efforts went into making the Dart body more acceptable to operators, and also making it fit Volvo's rival B6 which people at that stage expected to be far more successful than it proved to be in reality. By mid-1993, it was relaunched with gasket glazing and a front bumper that protected the windscreen. An order for 14 from then independent local operator Cambus, on troublesome B6 chassis, wasn't repeated, but Go Ahead was later persuaded to switch an order for 120 Dart bodies it might otherwise have placed with Wright and sales were picked up from other sources.

In 1995, the combined resources of the former Carlyle and Bedford businesses were deployed to develop the all-stainless steel Marshall Minibus, the country's first lowfloor rear-engined 25-seater. This owed at least a little inspiration to the much admired, but stillborn Bedford JJL which Marshall had built and helped develop 20 years earlier, and it secured some impressive initial orders from, among others, London General. Alas for Marshall, the Minibus's initial promise was let down by an apparently underpowered chassis with an incredibly noisy driveline. Its relaunch two years later might just have been too late to combat the challenge of Optare's cheaper and potentially more practical Solo.

Marshall had more success in transferring some of the Minibus's styling features on to the Dart body when it developed a lowfloor version, and it also worked with MAN and Iveco — the former enjoying fractionally more success than the latter, with larger single-deckers. Among its triumphs, it picked up a substantial order from CentreWest London Buses in 1997 for Dart SLFs, but with CentreWest and most other large independents joining big groups with supply contracts already negotiated with the likes of Plaxton, Wright and Alexander, its scope for growth was limited.

Two changes of name and at least one change of ownership were signs of an even more turbulent and troubled decade at Wadham Stringer, the Waterlooville, Hampshire coachbuilder better known before 1979 as the country's leading ambulance manufacturer and for its social services and military buses. It then enjoyed modest success with a perfectly acceptable looking PSV body called the Vanguard, especially as new chassis suppliers like Volvo, Scania and Dennis were eager to work with bodybuilders not already committed to meeting the needs of the established chassis makers.

Wadham Stringer was part of a motor dealership chain eventually absorbed into the Inchcape group which, by 1993, was selling off peripheral activities including the

Below:
The front lower panel and windscreens on the new-generation single-deckers from East Lancs were shared with the Pyoneer double-deck body. This is a Spryte, which uses the Alusuisse construction system pioneered in the UK by Wright. It is operated by Express Travel of Liverpool. SJB

coach works. Vanguard's sales had never grown big, even though it was adapted successfully to fit Leyland's short-lived Swift midibus. Wadham Stringer also was a competent, if relatively low volume competitor in the coachbuilt minibus market, and it also tried, to no great avail, to compete against the Plaxton Pointer with the Portsdown, a conventional steel body for the Dart.

Yet it displayed sufficient potential for Martyn Oldroyd and Tony McClellan to spend part of a recently won windfall on it in August 1993. In 1983, they were respectively Managing Director and Finance Director of a parcels company called Carryfast, and they teamed up with two fellow directors to buy that business from Unilever. Nine years later, the huge American UPS corporation made them an offer they couldn't refuse.

From then on they were bodybuilders, as UPS didn't want Customline Universal Vehicles, Carryfast's Dewsbury-based bodybuilding subsidiary and one of Wadham Stringer's competitors in the ambulance market. The road to Waterlooville became irresistible. They changed the company name to WS Coachbuilders as Inchcape retained the rights to the spelt-out version for its Wadham Kenning dealerships.

Oldroyd and McClellan formed the Universal Vehicles Group — UVG for short — which poured funds into reorganising the Waterlooville factory and developing new Cromweld-framed products including an updated Wessex minibus later renamed CityStar, a John Worker-designed Dart body called UrbanStar and the Dennis Javelin-based S320 coach. Ambulance production was transferred to Customline and WS was renamed UVG Bus Division.

Then they added another arm to UVG's activities by buying Bedwas, Securicor's coachbuilding subsidiary, and renaming it UVG Wales. Bedwas had grown from simply making its parent company's armoured vans into a van and social services welfare bus maker. Some of these activities overlapped those carried out at Waterlooville.

Meanwhile, in yet another attempt to crack the volume UK bus market, Mercedes started importing the O.405N, the lowfloor version of the bus bodied successively by Alexander, Wright and Optare. But instead of fitting a British body, it shipped all-steel vehicles built up to the shell stage on its own production line at Mannheim in Germany, and reduced the impact of high German labour costs by contracting UVG to paint and fit them out at Waterlooville. This also provided more opportunity for customers' representatives to monitor progress.

Things looked promising during the summer of 1997 when Travel West Midlands placed a pre-launch order for 100 O.405Ns for delivery in the first quarter of 1998. Despite that boost, UVG faced the same uphill struggle as Marshall in winning large body orders from big groups, while the ranks of independents more disposed to buying its products were becoming ever thinner. Everyone's truck-derived minibus sales were declining steadily, a large military order for Javelin coaches was coming to an end, and follow-up orders for the O.405N had yet to be secured.

By Christmas 1997, receivers were in at Waterlooville and looking for new owners, while UrbanStar production was suspended, CityStar production was transferred to Wales and all the stops were pulled out to complete the TWM Mercs and meet more limited demand for coaches.

The Waterlooville factory was bought by Caetano in the spring of 1998.

The decline in minibus sales brought other casualties in the 1990s. Dormobile stumbled to eventual oblivion and Robin Hood — which did well in the mid-1980s in partnership with Iveco — went through several changes of ownership and identity before re-emerging under its original name as a luxury coach manufacturer. Several others didn't even achieve that much presence.

The mainstream bus bodybuilders had cause to worry about the Mercedes/UVG deal as it showed that mainland European manufacturers could bypass them and supply this market from their huge production lines. The potential for this was increased in 1997 when Volvo added to its Scandinavian coachbuilding interests by acquiring Carrus Oy, a Finnish manufacturer turning out over 400 stainless steel bodies each year — 60% of them on Volvo chassis.

Were currency fluctuations to favour it, Volvo might be tempted to supply complete products into markets supplied by the major British bodybuilders — perhaps if mergers and takeovers created more pan-European bus and coach operators.

On the other hand, harmonious relationships like the Plaxton/Volvo partnership in North America show that the strongest bodybuilders and chassis makers can also work closely together for each other's mutual benefit and that the best organised bodybuilders have a healthy future ahead of them.

Below:
UVG ran into trouble at the end of 1997. Its range included the low-floor UrbanStar, seen here in service with Mackie of Alloa. Gavin Booth

THE LEON LINE

MICHAEL FOWLER looks at the workings of one of South Yorkshire's oldest-established family-run bus companies.

The village of Finningley, now in South Yorkshire but once divided between the West Riding and Nottinghamshire, has been home to Leon Motor Services for nearly 80 years. The original route was to Doncaster, and is still operated as the 191 with a few journeys extended daily to Misson (192) and on Tuesdays, Fridays and Saturdays to Wroot.

The company runs two Doncaster local services, the 195 to Warmsworth and the 196 to Hexthorpe. These were originally tendered operations. However, as a result of an increase both in frequency — from hourly to half-hourly — and in the hours of operation, currently from 8.30am to 6pm, these are no longer subsidised and have proved to be very popular.

An evening and Sunday service to Skellow via Toll Bar (152) from Doncaster's Northern Bus Station is operated commercially, as is route M89 serving a number of estates in West Bessacarr. This ran hourly for some time, but was increased to two buses an hour in 1997.

Two tendered routes from Doncaster were originally operated by Chesterfield Transport from its base in Bawtry, set up in 1988, but are currently worked by Leon on behalf of Stagecoach which took over the Chesterfield company in 1995. These are the 173 to Askern and the 174 to Sykehouse. The cost of the dead mileage from Bawtry had been prohibitive when the services were run by Stagecoach. Another tendered service is the circuitous route from Stainforth railway station to Hatfield Town End, the M85, which runs during the working day, Monday to Saturday.

Leon also runs locally in Scunthorpe.

The fleet of over 30 vehicles includes a large number of double-deckers. The route from Finningley to Doncaster serves two large comprehensive schools, for which high-capacity buses are required — Fleetlines and Atlanteans. The former RAF airbase has been closed and development plans are not yet finalised. The RAF married quarters, which were closed, have been sold as low-cost housing units and consequently traffic is now increasing. The vehicles used on regular service are fitted with Almex A90 electronic ticket machines.

Several Leyland Tiger coaches are used on a programme of excursions and tours operated from Doncaster South Bus Station and are very popular. The coaches are also used on private hire duties and on schools work.

My thanks go to Managing Director Tony Reece, Traffic Manager Eddie McGuiness and all the Leon staff with whom it has been my privilege to work on a part-time basis for very many years.

Below:
A former Scottish Bus Group Fleetline, with low-height ECW body, in Finningley. New in 1978 to Northern Scottish, it came to Leon via the Western Scottish fleet. It was one of three Western Fleetlines purchased in 1995. ALL PHOTOGRAPHS ARE BY THE AUTHOR

Right:
Double-deckers are needed for Leon's busiest routes. This 1977 Metro-Cammell-bodied Leyland Fleetline was new to the West Midlands PTE. Four were bought in 1990. Alongside it in the company's depot stands one of a pair of 1980 Alexander-bodied Fleetlines which came from AA Buses in 1988.

Below right:
At first sight looking like an ex-SBG Fleetline, this bus was bought new by Leon in 1980. Its Alexander body is to the same general specification as batches being built around the same time for Western Scottish and Midland Scottish — right down to the triangular destination display and the use of hopper vents in the side windows. It — and a similar W-registered ex-SBG bus — are the company's two most modern 'deckers.

Opposite above:
More recent new purchases have been two Dennis Darts with Plaxton Pointer bodies. The first was delivered in 1996. This one followed in the spring of 1997.

Opposite below:
A small number of Leyland Lynxes appeared on the secondhand market very quickly in the late 1980s and early 1990s. Leon snapped up a pair of two-year-old Southampton examples in 1991.

THE*LEON*LINE

Right:
The company's first new buses for some time were a pair of Optare MetroRiders which were purchased in 1994. One unloads shoppers in Hexthorpe.

Right:
Coaches carry the Leon Travel name. Underneath this Van Hool Alizee body is a Leyland Tiger chassis. New in 1984, it was bought by Leon in 1992. The location with the triffid-like lamp-posts is Calais.

Below:
A recent addition to the coach fleet has been this smart Tiger with Plaxton Paramount III body. It was new to Blackburn Transport. The buildings of Finningley airfield can be seen on the horizon.

YELLOW BUSES

MICHAEL H. C. BAKER reviews the operations of Yellow Buses of Bournemouth.

Public transport in seaside towns has always differed in several respects to urban transport inland, although in the past both were usually the prerogative of the local authority. Seaside bus fleets have to take account of huge seasonal variations; whilst the great majority of holidaymakers in the 1990s arrive in their own vehicles, many still come by train or coach and make use of local buses during their stay. There is also often a considerable number of retired people who rely on public transport. Yellow Buses, Bournemouth, is one of the relatively few companies still municipally owned. It will celebrate its centenary in 2002 and although it has certainly moved with the times its pattern and area of operations are typical of the traditional seaside town.

For a good many of its 90-odd years it co-existed happily with Hants & Dorset and its successor, Wilts & Dorset which operated long-distance services, leaving Bournemouth Corporation a clear field at home. However, privatisation changed all that and from 1987 onwards Bournemouth Transport has had to fight off a series of challengers. This it has successfully done and the future would seem to be a good deal more settled than the immediate past.

Perhaps the greatest change is in the type of vehicles likely to dominate the 127-strong fleet. 'What I'd like is a bendi-bus, the back half of which you could unhook outside the rush-hour.' Who knows, one day we may see such a vehicle on the streets of Bournemouth, for that is the ideal of Ted Reid, Managing Director of Yellow Buses. Of course no such bus exists at the moment and the bendi-bus has never really caught on in the UK. The bendi-tram has, and as Bournemouth was one of the last towns to give up electric traction, its trolleybuses disappearing in 1969, I asked Ted Reid if there were any plans to bring either trams or trolleys back. 'If someone cares to build a system down through the pedestrianised area in the centre of the town, over the Square, and up the other side, we'd be happy to run it for them, but I don't see any other possibility for light rail.'

Below:
Bournemouth pier around 1960, with a 1950 Titan PD2 on the left, a 1955 Tiger Cub in the centre, and a 1950 BUT six-wheel trolleybus on the right. Among the cars is a new Mini.
ALL PHOTOGRAPHS BY THE AUTHOR

Trams began operating in Bournemouth in 1902, though not, it has to be said, with any great enthusiasm. They had been inaugurated in the adjoining, and vastly more ancient, borough of Poole across the Dorset border the previous year, and it was only when the Poole & District Electric Traction Co, a subsidiary of BET, obtained permission to extend into Bournemouth, that Bournemouth Corporation woke up and obtained powers to build its own network. It then bought out the Poole company, Poole Corporation bought the track, leased it to Bournemouth, and the latter then took over operation of all the trams in both boroughs. So much for the beginnings.

Bournemouth is a most interesting town for it has grown from literally nothing 150 years ago to become one of the great (there are claims that it is the greatest) seaside resorts. The railway, the London & South Western, arrived in 1871 and was largely instrumental in its transformation. At that time the population was around 6,000; 10 years later it had trebled, and by the turn of the century when the trams began to operate, was approaching 60,000. Public transport has therefore always had a most important part to play in the history of the town.

I first met a Yellow Bus, or rather a yellow trolleybus belonging to Bournemouth Corporation Transport Services, the title the company assumed between May 1931 and March 1962, in the spring of 1944 when our family evacuated itself from our bombed and uninhabitable house in Croydon. Not only did I travel from the Central station to our flat close to the town centre in one, but each day took a number 25 to school at the Westbourne terminus. Only a few weeks ago I surprised myself by coming across a

piece of street furniture at Westbourne I had never noticed before embossed 'Bournemouth Corporation Tramways' almost hidden amongst bushes on a road I had driven and walked along a hundred times before.

A fleet of English Electric and Park Royal-bodied Sunbeam six-wheel trolleybuses, 102 in all, were put into service between 1934 and 1936, replacing all the trams in Bournemouth. They had already gone from Poole, apart from the Upper Parkstone Road route, the council entering into an agreement with Hants & Dorset who put a fleet of TD1 Leyland Titans into service in 1929. Bournemouth possessed the largest one-make fleet of trolleybuses to be found in any municipality in the UK, and it did Bournemouth proud, many of the Sunbeams giving the town over 20 years trouble-free service. There were several batches of trolleybuses delivered after the war, the very last arriving on 1 November 1962. This was a Weymann-bodied Sunbeam MF2B, No 301, registration 301 LJ. It had the distinction of being the last trolleybus built for operation anywhere in the United Kingdom. The almost silent running, clean, stately, primrose yellow trolleybuses seemed as integral a part of a resort which has always prided itself on its up-market gentility, as red buses in London, but Bournemouth could not fight the tide running through the nation and as it ebbed it took away Bournemouth's electrically powered double-deckers along with everyone else's. Their final day of normal operation was 19 April 1969, a grand funeral procession of no less than 17 trolleys, some preserved, taking place the following day, a Sunday.

Bournemouth had operated motorbuses for a long time, and although relatively few in number, many of them were distinctive and long-lived. A fleet of normal-control Bedfords was built up in the late 1930s, but war service saw many of them leave the town, never to return. Best remembered of all were 16 Leyland Titan TD5s with Weymann full-fronted bodies, delivered in 1939. They had sliding roofs and various other extras. They are the only Bournemouth Corporation motorbuses I can recall travelling on as a child, and they made a great impression on me, as they did on so many others. The entire batch served Bournemouth for well over 20 years, surely a record, the last one not retiring until 1965. Somewhat similar PD2s followed after the war; it was the PD3 which was initially chosen to replace the trolleys, 10 PD3A/1s with Weymann bodies arriving in 1963.

However, it was the Atlantean and the Daimler Fleetline which formed far and away the bulk of the trolleybus replacement fleet. The first with what might be termed the standard Bournemouth body, 10 MCW-bodied Atlanteans, Nos 170-9, were put into service in the latter part of 1964, and although these were withdrawn some years ago, there are still, as I write, 33 Fleetlines with similar Alexander bodies dating from 1979-81 in the Yellow Buses fleet. Bournemouth's very first rear-engined double-deckers were a pair of real curiosities, two Daimler Fleetlines with MH bodies, built in Belfast and intended for corporation service there. They arrived on the south coast in full Belfast Corporation maroon livery, but were repainted yellow before taking up work.

More Atlanteans and Fleetlines entered the fleet in the years 1964-9, the final 27 trolley-replacement Atlanteans of that year all having Alexander bodies, then a somewhat unusual make in southern England. Although subtly different to the earlier Weymann and MCW-bodied double-deckers they were generally similar, with plenty of stylish curves. The disappearance of the trolleybuses also signalled the coming end of two-man operation although it wasn't until 12 April 1986 that the last conductors hung up their bags and ticket machines.

Bournemouth's first Olympians introduced a new make of body, Marshall. Twenty of them, with fully automatic transmission, Nos 180-99, arrived in 1981/2. Marshall's participation in the double-deck field was short-lived. Bournemouth vehicles were to their standard 78-seat design, which with its pronounced taper to the upper deck windows was not a pretty sight.

Having arrived at vehicles which are part of the current fleet we ought to look at where they actually go. As Bournemouth spread during the latter part of the 19th century and through the 20th, so it swallowed up many older outlying hamlets and villages such as Boscombe, Winton, Kinson and Throop, and these became suburbs where lived many of those who found employment in the service industries in the town centre in hotels, department stores, theatres, restaurants, cinemas, the pier and so forth. Before long there was a continuous conurbation stretching from Poole to Christchurch Harbours. Brick-built terraced houses sprang up at the end of the 19th and the beginning of the 20th century, looking precisely like those found in dozens of other towns all over England, to be succeeded as more of the heathland disappeared between the two world wars by bow-windowed, mock Tudor semis with rising sun motifs on their garage gates. Whilst the better-off residents might have owned a Standard Flying Eight or a Hillman Minx, and the really wealthy, of whom there have always been plenty in Bournemouth, a chauffeur-driven Daimler, the vast majority of both residents and holidaymakers depended on public transport, and the trams, trolleybuses and motorbuses played a key role in the town's expansion in the 20th century.

The *Bournemouth Daily Echo* published on the Saturday before the 1938 August Bank Holiday recorded: 'Fleets of trolleybuses waited at both the West and Central Stations

and just after 5am the great invasion began.' Every available trolley and motorbus was pressed into service and 'rush' conductors were on duty at various strategic points to help out the regular conductors on particularly crowded vehicles.

Opposite:
A 1935 Park Royal-bodied Sunbeam MS2 illustrates Bournemouth's two-door layout at Bournemouth Pier. There were 84 buses in this order, a small number of which were still in operation in the early 1960s. A Burlingham-bodied Leyland Tiger can be seen in the background.

Above:
The first postwar double-deckers had full-width fronts. This is a 1950 PD2 with Weymann body — still with two doors, but now with just one staircase. It was one of 30.

Royal Blue operated coaches out of the lower floor of the unique two-storey bus and coach station beside the Square at Bournemouth. From 1934 Royal Blue had become part of Associated Motorways and by 1939 so many coaches belonging to Southdown, Midland Red, Timpsons, Greyhound and many other well known companies, as well as Royal Blue, were using the coach station and the stands around the Square, and the crowds they conveyed were so vast, that a contemporary report described the scene on a typical summer Saturday as 'general chaos'.

For a while after the end of World War 2 these halcyon days returned for public transport. It couldn't last and today the private car is a constant thorn in the side of Ted Reid's efforts to provide the public with the best possible bus service. I asked him about low-floor buses. Whilst he conceded they have their attractions, so would a bus with elastic sides which could squeeze in and out of the traffic and in particular draw up alongside stops which all too often, particularly in the summer, are blocked by residents who have just popped into a local shop. In the summer the population of Bournemouth doubles to around 300,000 and whilst this provides a big boost to Yellow Buses the extra

cars add to the traffic congestion. Several of Bournemouth's main shopping streets have been pedestrianised and on other town centre roads access is restricted to buses and taxis.

The Square (which is actually circular), at the bottom of Richmond Hill and spanning the River Bourne and its gardens — one of Bournemouth's greatest attractions — is the heart of Bournemouth. One of the corporation's favourite pastimes of late has been tinkering around with the layout of the Square, gradually increasing the space for pedestrians and reducing that for traffic, particularly private cars. Several times in recent years traffic flows around it have been altered so that one has never been quite sure quite where to stand if one has wanted to be run over by a bus, but through all these fascinating jigsaw puzzle variations, it (or rather the streets immediately adjoining it) has remained the principal terminus for Yellow Buses routes. Bournemouth's fine bus station was badly damaged by fire many years ago and has vanished, but as it was never used by corporation vehicles, it was only Hants & Dorset and coach services which were affected.

Various competitors appeared in both Bournemouth and Poole. In the former the greatest challenge came from a

fleet of minibuses, operated under the title of Charlie Cars, a revival of a name once familiar in the town. The striking Badgerline livery was also seen, as was the equally striking Barbara Windsor who launched the Bristol-based company's assault. All to no avail. The Badgers shuffled back to their Avon and Somerset setts in March 1988, and Charlie's Cars went out of business in October that year.

A new, high-profile competitor suddenly appeared in Bournemouth in the summer of 1993. A fleet of beautifully attired green and white Routemasters, which had operated for some years in Scotland after leaving London, began to work three routes, two of them to Christchurch from the Square, trading under the name of Bournemouth Heritage Transport Services and owned by Macvent Ltd. They were associated with the Bournemouth

Transport Museum, which kept its vehicles in the Yellow Buses depot at Mallard Road, and at least one of the former Corporation Daimler CR6Gs appeared in open-top form bearing the legend Hants & Dorset. Not surprisingly this venture into direct competition with Yellow Buses did not go down too well and the preserved fleet was asked to remove itself from Mallard Road. Accommodation was found at Hurn Airport.

Wilts & Dorset objected to the use of the Hants & Dorset name and this was dropped, being replaced by Routemaster Heritage. I travelled on the Routemasters several times, chiefly for the experience, but like many others I could not see them being a serious competitor to the long established Yellow Buses, not least because of the two-man crew, and also because I seldom saw any with more than a handful of passengers aboard. Choosing my words carefully I have to say the conductors were not always of the highest quality, whilst the all-Routemaster fleet soon began to be diluted with a variety of other very secondhand types, including some National single-deckers.

Yellow Buses fought back with a fleet of White Buses, a mixture of elderly repainted double-deckers from its own fleet and secondhand ones from various sources, including yet more London exiles, DMSs. It also bought four Bristol/ECW VRs from Yorkshire Traction, although these

latter were painted yellow. Both types had long been familiar in the town, operated by Wilts & Dorset; indeed the DMSs were former W&D vehicles, but their appearance in Yellow Buses livery took some getting used to. All were temporary additions to the fleet and have now been withdrawn.

Opposite above:
Between 1959 and 1963 Bournemouth added 30 Leyland Titan PD3s to its fleet, all with Weymann bodies. A preserved example, originally built with an enclosed top, is seen on sightseeing duties in 1996 in the company of an open-top Fleetline.

Opposite below:
From 1963 Bournemouth bought both Atlanteans and Fleetlines, and from 1969 these had Alexander bodies. In this view a solitary Fleetline, 111, is surrounded by Atlanteans.

Above:
Bournemouth town centre in the mid-1990s with from the left a 1979 Fleetline/Alexander, a 1990 Dominator/East Lancs and a Routemaster.

Framed in the front window of a Routemaster, a White Buses Fleetline with Yellow Buses on the front panel heads towards Bournemouth Square. The Fleetline was new to London Transport, reaching White Buses by way of Wilts & Dorset.

Below:
White Buses was part of the Yellow Buses operation. A White Buses Alexander-bodied Fleetline is followed by a Yellow Buses Leyland Olympian with Marshall body.

The Routemaster venture was subsidised from Scotland and when the parent group changed hands the new owners, discovering the loss the Bournemouth venture was making, quickly closed it down, a little over a year after it had started up.

There is another operator of double-deck buses — apart from Solent Blue Line which runs an express service between Bournemouth and Southampton — called Christchurch Buses. This, however, is a recently acquired subsidiary of Yellow Buses. Its small fleet consists of ex-Bournemouth Fleetlines and it operates contracts, two school services (which are both available to the general public) and the summertime Chines Tour open-top coastal service.

Ted Reid quite reasonably is not prepared to discuss the profitability of routes for commercial reasons, but it is no secret that the series of routes which link the Square with Boscombe and Christchurch have always been the biggest money-spinners for Bournemouth Corporation with a bus every few minutes, whilst even after 6pm weekday, and on Sundays there are six buses an hour.

In all Yellow Buses operates 34 routes, including the three summertime tours and the two express services, the once-a-day X22 from Somerford and the X8 from the town centre to Bournemouth International Airport, better known to the locals as Hurn. This is a once-daily service which connects with Ryan Air flights to and from Dublin.

Although owned by Bournemouth Corporation, Yellow Buses, with an independent board of directors, operates on a commercial basis and has fought hard since 1987 to maintain and indeed expand its business.

Since the demise of the Routemaster venture peace has broken out, more or less, in Bournemouth. There is still some competition Yellow Buses is quite prepared to challenge Wilts & Dorset for contract work but otherwise the two big players on the Bournemouth scene appear content to keep their long-established spheres of influence. Just one Yellow Buses route, the 30, penetrates Poole town centre, but even this is not in direct competition for it avoids Bournemouth town centre, its eastern terminus being Boscombe Pier which it reaches by way of suburban Winton, Wallisdown, where the vastly expanded Bournemouth University is situated, Alderney and Poole Hospital.

Ten services are supported by Dorset County Council. In April 1997 Bournemouth became a unitary authority and Dorset retreated westwards to Poole's western boundary but the services continue to be supported by Bournemouth, at least until the present agreement runs out.

I asked Ted Reid about school contracts — I had made the mistake of travelling to Mallard Road on the upper deck of a bus which had contained a number of appallingly loud-mouthed children — and he said that although they do not make anyone's fortune, by taking them on they discourage other operators who might be tempted to muscle in on Yellow Buses routes rather than keep their vehicles idle between 9.30am and 3pm.

The seafront service, operated from May to September by a fleet of nine open-top 1978-vintage Alexander-bodied Fleetlines marketed under the title 'Windjammers', is highly profitable and, much as Guide Friday would like a share, Ted Reid is determined to keep it a Yellow Buses monopoly. The 1¼hr ride (Yellow Buses' longest regular journey) from Christchurch Quay to Sandbanks, where Wilts & Dorset open-top Olympians take the ferry to Studland and Swanage, is most attractive, with extensive views across the bay to the Isle of Wight and the Purbeck Hills. The route takes the buses down roads, or 'chines' as Bournemouth likes to call pine-covered valleys leading to the sea, some of them full of hotels and boarding houses erected before it occurred to anyone that double-deck buses might venture down them, and with cars parked on either side Yellow Buses drivers need infinite patience and an ability to judge precisely how many half centimetres they have to spare on either side. But then they are hand-picked and having just ridden from Sandbanks to the Square I can vouch for their remarkable skill at keeping to time even on scorching high summer Sundays when most of southern England seems to have decided to head for the Dorset coast.

Relations with the preservationists have been repaired to the extent that a Routemaster now wears Yellow Buses livery and various vintage open-top vehicles, now back at Mallard Road, work route 11, the summer-only town tour, advertised in the Bournemouth Transport timetable as 'Vintage Yellow Buses'. It occurred to me that at least one of these, the 1965 Weymann-bodied Fleetline for instance, there was little apart from its original maroon and green stripes and fleetname that would enable the ordinary holidaymaker to spot that this was a 31-year-old preserved vehicle. This, I guess, is a comment either on how advanced it was when it entered service or how little things had moved on in the design of double-deckers in the subsequent 13 years. A former Portsmouth Corporation Metro-Cammell-bodied Atlantean of 1966 has also worked open-top services, as well as a far more obviously vintage half-cab former Bournemouth Corporation PD3 and an ex-Maidstone & District AEC Regal.

Which brings us to the subject of liveries. The trams were adorned in a typically ornate lined-out maroon and yellow. The latter became the dominant colour when the trolleybuses took over and remains so to this day, which seems entirely appropriate for a select south coast resort; well I mean, black and dark grey would look a little bizarre, wouldn't it? When I was at art college, along with Rembrandt and Whistler's mother, it was drummed into us that 'red and green should never be seen', but the thin green lining edging the thicker maroon stripes sets off the basic yellow of Bournemouth's buses and trolleys very nicely. The town's coat of arms was evidence of ownership and fleet numbers were in an ornate shaded serif. There was a strict policy of no exterior advertisements and the general effect was one of considerable style and dignity. In 1973 the maroon and green began to disappear, sadly, whilst a new motif inside a blue circle with 'go faster' (though they didn't actually) blue flashes replaced the coat of arms.

The need to find new sources of revenue meant exterior advertisements now appeared on Bournemouth buses. Fleet numbers were reduced to very small sans serif.

It cannot be said that these changes were for the better. In 1982 the blue bits disappeared, being replaced by 'Yellow Buses' (or 'Coaches') in well proportioned brown lettering with a stripe underneath incorporating 'Bournemouth' in small letters. This was altogether better. For long known locally as 'The Yellows', 'Yellow Buses, Bournemouth' became the official trading name of the company at this time.

The Ted Reid regime coincided with another change, blue returning with a vengeance, this time in the form of a broad band along the lower panels and on the roof. Lettering, although the style stayed the same, also became blue. All-over adverts have become an increasingly noticeable feature in Bournemouth, but through it all yellow has predominated, making a Bournemouth bus instantly recognisable. An attractive interior feature of modern Bournemouth buses is the seat moquette which is blue and yellow, the pattern made up of Ys and Bs.

Although Bournemouth has operated minibuses from time to time, none presently features in the fleet. Ted Reid sees little future for them in Bournemouth. 'Minibuses need mini wages to make them pay; if you carry only one or two passengers on one journey you need virtually a full load on the next one to break even.'

Yellow Buses pursues a very different vehicle policy to Wilts & Dorset. The latter's large fleet of MetroRiders is a familiar sight in Bournemouth; the Nationals have now all gone, largely replaced by six DAF Deltas which entered service in 1993. By contrast, although the 75th Bournemouth Corporation anniversary booklet, published in 1977, listed some six minibuses and eight full-size single-deckers, 10 years later the only single-decker still featured was No 55, a Roadliner which by then was preserved by the museums department. Bournemouth bought 11 Willowbrook-bodied Daimler Roadliners in 1967/8, but like most other operators found them a disappointment and they did relatively little work.

For some years Yellow Buses was an all double-deck fleet. There was a four-year gap after the delivery of the Marshall-bodied Olympians, then in 1986 came the company's first Volvos. These were five Volvo B10M-50 Citybuses with distinctive East Lancashire 76-seat coach bodies, Nos 200-204. Only one is now officially listed as a coach; the rest are listed under the bus fleet although they retain their high-back coach-type seats.

There is one other double-deck coach in the current fleet, No 1, a Scania K112 with Berkhof 74-seat body, new in 1987 and purchased in May 1995. Nos 200-4 were

followed in 1988-9 by 10 more Volvos, this time fitted with Alexander RH 80-seat bus bodies.

Ted Reid took over at Bournemouth in October 1989 and this signalled another change in chassis preference, 18 Dennis Dominators with East Lancashire bodies, arriving in 1990-2. Mr Reid began his career as a Traffic Clerk with Burnley, Colne & Nelson Joint Transport in 1954 stayed there for 19 years left to become a newsagent for 18 months, 'disillusioned by the fact that various people came and went in positions such as the Traffic Superintendent without any possibility of myself or others within my department being given the opportunity to fill such a post'; but with 'diesel in my veins', Ted Reid soon returned to the industry and was Deputy Managing Director of Hull City Transport immediately before moving to Bournemouth.

It looks like the Dominators may be Bournemouth's last double-deckers, at least for the foreseeable future, for like so many other operators, single-deckers now seem to be the order of the day. They are still relatively few in number, 28, and there will no doubt remain a need for double-deckers on school services and during peak hours, but to quote Ted Reid, his elderly passengers regard a double-decker 'as merely a 33-seat single-decker', for they are not able to climb upstairs.

In 1993 the first more or less full-sized single deckers since the Roadliners arrived in the shape of six East Lancashire-bodied 48-seat, 17-standing Dennis Lances, Nos 401-6. Twelve buses with similar 40-seat, 16-standing bodies on 9.8m Dart chassis, Nos 451-62, were delivered in 1995, and 10 more similar buses, Nos 463-72, were put into service in 1996.

Although Bournemouth has always had a small fleet of single-deck coaches — for instance, three distinctive full-fronted Burlingham-bodied Leyland PS1s were delivered in 1949, and all still exist in preservation — the 1990s had seen an enormous expansion in this field. A number of

Plaxton-bodied Leyland Leopards and Tigers were bought for private hire use in the 1970s and 1980s, but in April 1992 the purchase of Dorset Travel Services meant that Yellow Buses was now a player of some significance in National Express. This fleet is, however, quite separate from the Yellow Buses one. In Yellow Coach livery there are nine full-size coaches: four DAFs, three Scanias, and two Leyland Tigers. Bodywork is by Plaxton, Irizar and Van Hool. There are also three mini-coaches: two Talbot Express 14-seaters and one 18-seat Toyota Optimo 2.

Currently there are some 30 coaches in National Express livery, based at Mallard Road. Ted Reid is not altogether happy with the present National Express set-up. 'There isn't sufficient profit for operators, we need to be given a sensible increase to make a long-term commitment.'

National Express has to operate on very tight profit margins. As Ted Reid put it: 'Students and pensioners are our chief customers; you don't get businessmen travelling National Express.'

Opposite:
Recent deliveries to Yellow Buses have been Dennis Darts with East Lancs bodies. This is a 1996 bus. From 1997 the company switched to the low-floor Dart SLF.

Above:
Dorset Travel Services is part of the Bournemouth Transport business, operated separately from the Yellow Buses fleet. A Volvo B10M with Plaxton Premiere 350 body to Expressliner specification loads in Bath on its way to Blackpool in the summer of 1996.

Mallard Road depot itself is an impressive building. The corporation has had a number of depots over the years, but gradually Mallard Road has replaced them all; the former tram depot at Pokesdown almost opposite the station survived as a secondhand furniture showroom until a year or so ago. Mallard Road garage and workshops were officially opened on 24 July 1953, and subsequent extensions on the 24-acre site have meant that it has been the company's sole depot, repair facility and head office since the beginning of 1968.

The future for Bournemouth would seem to lie with the single-decker. Ted Reid's most recent thoughts make that quite clear: 'we have had a policy recently whereby we have purchased more cost-effective (ie Dennis Dart midibuses) and utilised these vehicles on the marginal routes.' They particularly come into their own on winter Sundays when the double-decker almost goes into hibernation. More double-deckers are to be replaced and 'in making this decision we will of course examine the low-floor type of vehicle'. These appeared in 1997 as Dennis Dart SLFs, with East Lancashire Spryte bodies.

As yet Bournemouth has no bus lanes, unlike neighbouring Poole, but they are certainly needed and Yellow Buses is 'currently in discussion with the Local Authority on the possible provision of (these)'.

Apart from the two double-deck and 12 single-deck coaches, there are currently 28 single-deck buses in the fleet, the oldest dating from 1993. There are 85 double-deckers, the oldest dating from 1976, the newest from 1992. It will be interesting to see how this proportion changes in the future.

Above:
Open-toppers looking for business at Bournemouth Pier in 1995. Both are Fleetlines, the one in the background being a preserved 1965 model.

Below:
View from the top! A Yellow Buses Fleetline provides a grandstand view of the seafront at Poole in the summer of 1996.

Lewis LEGENDS

Lewis is a bit off the beaten track for most bus photographers, but ROY MARSHALL has made a number of trips to the island. This selection of views spans two decades of change, from the mid-1950s to the mid-1970s.

...ot widely publicised was the restricted availability during World War 2 of ...series Austins with 19-seat Scottish Commercial bodies. They were few in ...umber. Western Lewis Coaches operated one which, judging by the destination ...splay, was permanently allocated to the service from Stornoway to Shawbost.

...L PHOTOGRAPHS BY THE AUTHOR

Below:
A rather more modern Duple-bodied Victor, in service with Hebridean Transport in 1968. This style of Duple body was most commonly associated with Bedfords but was also built on small numbers of Albions and Leyland Comets.

Below, top to bottom:

The standard small wartime bus was the Bedford OWB with 32-seat utility bodywork by Duple or SMT. New in 1943 and bodied by SMT, this OWB was originally operated by W. Alexander & Sons. It was sold to Western Lewis Coaches in 1948 and fitted with 28 coach seats.

Hebridean Transport operated this Duple-bodied Albion Victor, photographed in Stornoway bus station in 1959.

A 1945 OWB, purchased by Mitchell of Stornoway from SMT in 1948, and seen in Stornoway's bustling harbour six years later.

Above:

Two oddities which found their way to Lewis, and both owned by Lochs Motor Transport. Nearest the camera is the only Albion Viking VK41L to have operated in Britain. The VK41L had a front-mounted Leyland engine and this one, with Alexander Y-type body, was originally a demonstrator running for Alexander (Midland). Alongside stands a Dodge S306, one of two demonstrators built in 1962. This one had a Weymann body. The grille is made up of parts from the contemporary Dodge truck range. These two unique buses were photographed in 1968.

Right:

The first 36ft-long bus on the island was this Bedford VAL operated by Mitchell — whose 15-strong fleet was at this time 100% Bedford. New in 1964, it had a 51-seat body by Duple (Midland). Bus-bodied VALs were relatively uncommon.

Below:

Many of Mitchell's buses had registrations with triple numbers such as GJS 888, a 1960 Bedford SB1 with 43-seat Duple (Midland) body. Its sister vehicle was GJS 777. The SB1 had a 300cu in Bedford diesel engine. Its virtue was economy. Its vice was noise.

Left:
For most of the 1960s and into the 1970s somewhat utilitarian Bedford buses were the standard fare on Lewis. This is a 1958 C5Z1 with Duple (Midland) body operated by Mitchell of Stornoway, who was the local Vauxhall agent.

Right:

A later and more mundane Lochs Motor Transport bus is this one-time MacBrayne Bedford VAS1 with Duple (Midland) body. New in 1962, it passed to Highland Omnibuses in 1970 as that operator gradually took over the bulk of MacBrayne's bus operations. It was bought by Lochs Motor Transport in 1973, and served them until 1982.

Below:

Bedford buses continued to be favoured by Mitchell, as illustrated by a 1977 SB with body by Willowbrook, successors to Duple (Midland). The livery has improved, with cream window surrounds as well as a cream waistband, to lighten the dark blue used by Mitchell. Distinctive registrations were still favoured. This was one of a pair registered KJS 444R and KJS 555R. The body on this SB is little different from that on GJS888 of almost 20 years earlier which is illustrated on the previous page.

By Slow Stages to a Service

ROBERT E. JOWITT, travelling by stage carriage to the memorial service of a worthy man, harks back to a paparazzo past with a lovely girl and long-vanished coaches; and while failing almost entirely to emulate the conversational successes of a famous present-day travel writer, manages to capture the efforts of other travellers in his own typical recording of this unlikely journey.

Elderly readers and purchasers of secondhand bus books may recall that in *Buses Annual 1983*, in an article entitled 'Birmingham Sessions, Impressions and Digressions', one of the digressions is on Leicester in 1973 where 'I am able to photograph the buses' and 'discover a very beautiful girl' and send the girl 'some prints of the photos I take of her…and these are the only pictures of Leicester that I ever bother to print, the rest just remaining negatives doubtless acquiring great historic value and possibly to appear in *Buses Annual 1999* if I and it still survive at that date…'.

It, as *Buses Yearbook*, and I, name unchanged, still do, so obviously I have to include a couple of photographs of Leicester in this present volume. I do not intend, however, to write about the buses of Leicester (on which other authors are better qualified to dwell) nor to write of the beautiful Norleen Bensley whom, though I remember her with great fondness, I have never seen or heard of from that day to this.

Moreover, before I remembered that I was supposed to be putting photos of Leicester in *Buses Yearbook 1999* I had already been inspired to go back far beyond the Norleen romance for a suitable subject for this momentous date. Thus Leicester remains now, as it did in 1983, a digression, and I shall now continue from where I really intended starting.

Donny Dewdeney was gathered to his forefathers at the ripe old age of four score years; I chanced to espy the notice in the personal columns of *The Times*. Announcement of a memorial service would follow in due course.

Right:
It was hinted in *Buses Annual 1983* that Jowitt photographs of Leicester in 1973 would appear in *Buses Annual 1999*. The 'Annual' may now be a 'Yearbook', but as good as his word here is a representative example, with a Midland Red D9 partially obscured — in classic Jowitt fashion — by a group of mainly female pedestrians.
ALL PHOTOGRAPHS ARE BY THE AUTHOR

Some three and a half decades earlier, between 1958 and 1961, my multifarious photographic interests had included his teenage daughter Julia. Let me say here, for fear that anyone, however unreasonably, may cast stones of misrepresentation or suchlike, that the names I am giving are not the real names. This device is often used in the agony tales in women's magazines. So I am assured.

Donny Dewdeney and my father were acquainted over archaeological matters of mutual interest. My father was secretary of the local field club, and Donny D was a mighty man of valour in the preservation of fauna and flora; thus Julia and I moved — and danced — in the same social orbit, a world of polite dances long since trampled underfoot by the onslaught of discos. Waltzes, quicksteps, eightsome reels and, as an occasional concession to youth, cha-cha-cha and rock'n'roll.

In the autumn of 1958, in one of several letters from boarding school, along with details of being the dormitory senior having to stop six of the naughtiest juniors running upstairs two-at-a-time she added, knowing my interests: 'These are the names of coaches and buses I saw on the way back from Wales: United Welsh, South Wales, Red & White, Black & White, Western Welsh, N&C Express, Rhondda, F. N. Morgan, T. Davies, Bebbs, Victoria of Treorchy, Merthyr Tydfil Corporation, Rambling Rose, Howells, Bryn, Marchants, Silver Star, Shamrock & Rambler, Don Everall…'

In schoolgirl hand, magic names from a golden past age! She must have been quite fond of me to write them all down. I was quite fond of her, too, judging by the number of photographs I took of her — Julia in diverse glamorous ball gowns, Julia in a longish fawn-coloured overcoat she often wore when out walking, Julia with Shandy her golden retriever, Julia, Julia, photo after photo.

Towards the end of the period I fell much under the influence of Fellini's *La Dolce Vita* and, invariably equipped with camera and flashgun, fancied myself in the role of

paparazzo. I had some hopes of becoming a society photographer, though the equipment was more often used for buses and trams and, with hindsight, I am rather glad I did not pursue the career.

I remember one Dolce Vita night taking photos of Julia dancing with this chap at a party, then driving my sister and her boyfriend home in our Ford Prefect and hotly pursuing a Southampton Corporation Guy, *en route* no doubt to a scrapyard up north, overtaking it twice to stop ahead and flash it, a pursuit much enjoyed by sister and boyfriend despite their lack of interest in Southampton Guys; and then returning to the party — now moved to Julia's house, and flashing Julia dancing somewhat closer with this chap.

In truth, Julia and I intermittently talked about 'going steady' and I drove her here and there in the Ford Prefect and occasionally quite illegally let her drive it — it was actually my father's — and I was sufficiently attached to her to take Shandy for walks when his mistress couldn't come too. There were ever other stars on both our horizons. Julia's and mine, that is; I cannot speak (or bark) for Shandy.

Had I but known it, our own particular star was about to crash below the horizon. I had stuck all the photos of Julia in an album, Julia begged to borrow it, Julia's mummy 'discovered it' (as the play-writers say) and took exception to the (perfectly innocent) contents. Were some of the photos too provocative, were there too many of them, had I perhaps set up the album in too Dolce Vita a style? Mrs D, whose short temper over trifles I had already encountered, demanded that I give her all the negatives.

I replied politely but firmly that I never parted with my negatives.

'Give me the negatives!' Mrs D repeated, 'or you shall never cross this threshold again!' Or words to that effect.

I never did cross the threshold again. The year 1961 was curious, not least because if you turned the numbers upside down they still said the same date; but my life

turned upside down, for I largely abandoned the world of society dances for art student jazz hops. Donny Dewdeney and my father, either ignorant or dismissive of the photographic episode, remained on good archaeological terms until the Dewdeneys left the area, by which time Julia and I had long lost track of each other.

And so 35 years later, again by sheer chance, I noticed in *The Times* the announcement of Donny Dewdeney's memorial service, to be held in Bath Abbey. My own respect for his works coupled with my now long-dead father's regard for him convinced me that I should attend the service. I must admit I hoped I might catch a glimpse of Julia too.

The family Ford Fiesta being required for family purpose, I decided to travel by bus, and to write of my experiences on the journey for *Buses Yearbook*; starting from the far northwest of Herefordshire it could prove quite a trek!

I start off slightly on the wrong foot by neglecting to ascertain if the Teme Valley term-time-only 802 is running. As a schools bus driver myself I know my own Primrose Travel bus is still enjoying its holidays, but the 802 is a college bus, and perhaps Hereford College is starting again this very Monday. I am not prepared to walk a mile only to find out at 7.45am that it isn't, so I avail myself of a lift in the family Fiesta as far as Leominster.

Here Primrose Bedford 181, known as the Tin Can, is due to depart at 9.20am on the 501 to Hereford. So it starts up and starts buzzing and doesn't stop buzzing and doesn't start out. Vital minutes tick by, then replacement appears in the form of ex-Northern of Sheffield ex-somewhere else Leyland semi-automatic 'Happy', known thus for its numberplate HPY. I have driven Happy myself sometimes, on schools and on the Saturday 501.

In undue time we set off. As I am intending to write a traveller's tale I feel I ought to be engaging in conversation, in Paul Theroux fashion, with everyone I meet. Apart from telling the driver — who has not driven Happy before — the difference between the button for shutting the door and the button for cutting out the engine — rather too late — conversation in Theroux style does not prove possible, for the only other passenger is a lady near the back plainly angry at the delay.

Halfway along the route Fred gets on. I often take Fred into Hereford on a Saturday 501, for the purpose, I suspect, of inspecting Hereford hostelries. Fred looks mildly surprised to see me sitting on the wrong side of the bus, on a Monday morning.

'Hello, Fred,' I say. 'Nice morning.'

'Yes,' he agrees. I notice he is wearing overalls.

'Keeping busy?' I ask in a spirit of friendly enquiry.

'Yes, well…' He shrugs his shoulders perhaps he has a headache.

Then Jenny gets on. I have reproved Jenny in the past for forgetting her college bus pass. That's how I know her name is Jenny. Delightful girl though she is, I feel that engaging in Theroux-style conversation with her might be misinterpreted.

Then we pass the Teme Valley 802 coming back from Hereford…

Now as we approach Hereford I realise that if I stay aboard until the bus station I will miss my connection, so I abandon Primrose and walk across a segment of Hereford to head off the next bus on its way out after it has left the bus station. This is VPR 862X, a trim 35-seater of H&H Coaches, Ross-on-Wye. Apart from the driver it is empty, and I ask him if it is usually so; he replies in a pleasant Herefordshire accent that there's sometimes one or two. One girl gets on at Wormelow Tump, otherwise nobody, and she doesn't look as if she will engage in Theroux conversation, and the driver is busy with the gradients, so, apart from the engine, silence reigns. We travel up and down over country like a tablecloth thrown wantonly in rumples with white sugar-lumps of farms tossed here and there on its surface, then descend a dramatic pine-clad gorge to Monmouth.

Having explored Monmouth some 10 years ago and watched buses passing over Monnow bridge and through the Monnow Gate I decide not to tarry; disregarding the vintage charm of Soudley Valley Leyland Dominant GBB 999N, no doubt shortly to wander into Forest of Dean delights, I board my next bus — having failed to photograph it coming through the Monnow Gate, but never mind, as I probably took a similar one 10 years ago.

This one is Stagecoach Red & White Leyland Paramount AAX 450A — it can't really be that old — and the driver is a young man with a pony-tail. The route, after crossing the Wye, does a grand tour of a 1950s council estate designed with neither parked cars nor moving 36ft-long buses in mind; the combination of both means we waggle in and out and on and off the kerb at distressingly frequent intervals, and all just for two passengers to descend. Which leaves three.

One old lady gets out at Redbrook only a youth and myself remain throughout. The youth is engaged with his Walkman; not wishing to interrupt him I concentrate on the scenery. These are very beautiful reaches of the Wye Valley, the road sometimes on ledges high above the river; the sort of place where you hope the driver is very good and wish the bus wouldn't make that nasty clonking noise. I am sitting right at the rear, just for a change, and I notice that the backs of the headrests are furnished in at least six different styles, one of them signed by Zoe, Sara et al. As Zoe and Sara are not here today — though they probably wouldn't speak to me if they were, nor I to them — I compose descriptions of the cottages and gardens of Llandogo and Tintern assuming an almost Dordogne aura in the bright April morning.

Arriving in Chepstow I wander along streets laid out in an interesting gridiron pattern and abounding in chip shops; but I buy a pastie in a pie shop and a pint in a pub. I observe a Leyland National on a local route from Bulwark to Beachley; the route must be four or five miles long but the termini are only a mile apart, on either side of the mouth of the Wye.

According to my usual habit I photograph this bus with a girl in the foreground perhaps she is Zoe or Sara but I fail to photograph it going through the town gate, because whenever it does this I happen to be in pie shop or pub, and then it is time to board the Badgerline Mercedes with driver speaking in suitable Somerset accent. As it pulls out I see a French coach negotiating the city gate but under the circumstances I fail to photograph that too.

So, over the Severn Bridge, and then past Filton aerodrome where half-a-dozen elderly airliners are parked in a row like secondhand cars, for all the world as if you could go in and buy one. Perhaps you can. Then an architectural study of the seven ages of spreading Bristolian suburbia, and at last Bristol itself.

Some years have elapsed since I last photographed Bristol buses, so I spend a couple of exhausting hours making up for this, though I find the Bristol fashions for young ladies of today less attractive than those on my earlier visits.

I then head for Bath on Badgerline VR5544 (EWS 752W) with a warning from the driver that it is likely to be late and diverted. This proves to be the case. Near Saltford the driver of a Badgerline coming the other way takes both hands off the wheel to make a magnificent gesture of the road still being blocked. We then crawl in a queue for a very long time while trains sail past mockingly on the main line.

As we start onto the diversion we actually see the cause, a large artic overturned and its load of chipboard sheets spread across the highway. The bus crawls up fearsome hills to a place called Twerton, then rushes down fearsome hills into Bath. I have less time than I would have had to photograph buses and girls in Bath bus station before catching a minibus to the house of a friend where I am staying; at which, nevertheless, I arrive at the appointed hour and can then relax with his library which very properly includes a shelf of *Buses Annuals* and *Yearbooks*…

In the morning I do an architectural perambulation and study the ways of the open-top sightseeing buses, before descending to the Abbey. 'Descending' is quite a proper word to use in connection with Bath Abbey, for on the west front are carvings of Jacob's Ladder with angels ascending and descending, the descent of the latter being portrayed by their coming down head first.

I must of course refrain from saying anything about the memorial service, save that Mrs D does not recognise me in the multitude and I would not have recognised her had I not known who she was. Julia however, apart from looking somewhat older, has the same hairstyle and the same sort of fawn coat as she had in one of my more decorous, if less decorative, photographs.

Afterwards, outside, below the angels descending, the congregation reassembles. A specimen of Bath's famous

Above:
We move on, *appasionata*, to Bath bus station, with Badgerline buses with closed doors.

Right:
Moments of relief from the constant passing of Bristol City Line buses are provided by, for example, this A-Bus ex-Hampshire Bus Bristol VRT. The VRT in the background belongs to another City Bus competitor — Swift Link.

Opposite:
Bath Abbey, rising magnificently in the background, was really the author's destination. The sight of a City Tour Fleetline in the foreground, though decidedly old, was merely a bonus.

poor wanders round the fringes of the well-dressed throng repeating loudly: 'Are you going to vote Labour?' but they are too busy talking to each other and to Julia to pay him any heed. I do not speak to Julia myself for fear she might deem it tactless. I just think about her driving the Ford Prefect one night, she devoid of licence and scrunching the gears horribly; and I wonder if she remembers.

I retire to the Saracen's Head. Here I really do have a Conversation, with a youth repairing the fruit machine, seeing as I and my pint happen to be sitting right next to it. He tells me that one evening he had to go to Twerton — and obeying the rules of give and take in conversation I say that I was there yesterday evening — in order to mend a pool table. Him, that was, you realise; I just went through Twerton on a bus. Anyway, it was his last call of the evening and lots of chaps were waiting to play pool and a couple of days later he had to go back to mend the pool table again because the chaps had had a terrific punch-up about who would have first go on the pool table and smashed up not only the pool table but the entire pub. Then he departs to attend to his next fruit machine and I return to the sightseeing buses, and sightseeing French girls who seem to make up half the population of Bath.

I expect to see some English girls too. I don't see Julia again, but then I didn't really think I would. When the afternoon is waning and for perhaps the 17th time I walk past the lady who is persuading people to ride on Guide Friday buses, she says to me: 'You have been having a busy day, haven't you!'

'Yes, I certainly have,' I agree. One way and another she's quite right, and it isn't finished yet. In the evening my host and I attend a lecture, brilliant and witty, given by my good friend Peter Davey on Bristol Tramways, on which subject he is the acknowledged expert.

On Wednesday morning I have the choice of returning via my outward route or travelling in my host's car to Cheltenham where he is due at a meeting. I choose the latter, and we head up the A46. Just beyond Stroud we overtake a Peterborough Bus Co VR heading for Gloucester. The unwonted nature of this spectacle and the topic of Stagecoach vehicle swaps prove so engrossing that it occurs to neither of us until some time after we have turned off its route that I could have caught a Peterborough bus to Gloucester, this being where I intend going. In the event I catch a Gloucester Stagecoach bus from Brockworth; it is so modern and boring that I take no details of it at all.

Gloucester at 10am is far from lively, but the dingy purlieus of the bus station are enhanced, just as I hoped, by the fairly frequent passage of fairly elderly independents in many hues. By midday the scene is starting to acquire some animation but I decide I have had enough of it and catch a Red & White on the 38 for Ross-on-Wye.

The bus is AAX 410A, in about the same condition as her sister two days ago. The driver is the first I encounter, in 35 years of bus photography, who says I ought to ask his permission before photographing his bus; but he may be trying to be funny, as he ends up saying he does not want his wife to know where he is. Incidentally he has receding hair at the front and a pony-tail at the back. I

begin to wonder if pony-tails are part of Stagecoach uniform. I do not believe I was photographing his bus anyway; I think I was photographing a Soudley Valley Leyland, slightly younger than the example I saw two days ago, with a Japanese girl walking past it.

We crawl through Gloucester and speed along the Roman road westwards, the humps of the Forest of Dean rising ahead and the unmistakable clump-clad summit of May Hill to the right. Leaving the Roman road the route turns northwest across a corner of the Forest of Dean where cottages nestle picturesquely and almost impossibly on steep tree-clad slopes and the hedges and orchards are brilliant with blossom. Whatever his views on bus photography, our driver handles the endless bends in fine style.

At Ross-on-Wye there is no bus station, just some white marks in a nondescript street with the unlikely name of Cantilupe Road. A cantilupe, if I recall correctly, is some sort of melon. A fine iron sign with a black pointing hand tells you that the public conveniences are 150yd away; I cannot vouch for the truth of this for I walk about 100yd in a different direction to the ancient town hall on stone pillars. From here I see AAX heading down the hill for Hereford and I sit in the sun for 45min hoping to see the opposite working. This idleness is very pleasant but quite unprofitable, for either because of roadworks, or because it always goes another way, the opposite working fails to materialise.

I return to Cantilupe Road, where a Leyland National is sunning itself in bored and boring fashion, and an elderly gent gives me the opinion that the bus for Hereford is late. I assure him that it isn't, for the town hall clock has only just struck two; we discover that he is looking at the wrong half of the timetable.

The bus actually comes in on time, a Red & White ex-

West Midlands Titan WDA 2T and looking a bit sad. The driver is a middle-aged man with a mane and a pony-tail. I follow the elderly gent and his two young grandsons upstairs. The boys sit in the front offside seat, grandad behind them. I sit in the third nearside; there is a fair-haired girl in the front nearside. The boys peer down the periscope and declaim loudly about the driver getting out, a new driver getting in, and how this new one is going bald. He hasn't a pony-tail either.

The bus meanders around the edge of Ross, lending some weight to my theory that there are roadworks and confusion. As it crosses the Wye grandpa feeds the boys with biscuits, then the younger one falls asleep. Grandpa warns the older one not to let little brother fall off the seat. The girl says: 'Come and sit here if you like so you can keep an eye on him.' So grandpa does, with alacrity, and proves to be quite as gifted as Paul Theroux in the art of conversation with strangers on public transport.

By the time we reach Kings Thorn summit, which affords a higher viewpoint over that delectable tablecloth of farmland with its sugar-lump farmhouses mentioned on the outward journey, and Hereford is in sight in the distance, we have heard all about his wife's angina and the reasons he spends a lot of time taking his grandsons about. And more: we know the girl comes from Aberystwyth, she is working near Ross where her boyfriend lives, her name is Rhondda Perry — 'Perry, that's a good drink!' says grandpa — and she is 22 years old — 'I'd have said you were 19!' says grandpa gallantly, to which she coyly replies 'Some people think I'm 16!' — and she has two horses at home in Aberystwyth but she wants to move them nearer to Ross. By the time we get off the bus in Hereford grandpa has Rhondda's address, in order that he can make arrangements for her to keep her horses in his son's field.

After a long wait at the bus station and the incidental arrival of WDA 1T and later another AAX driven by what looks like the same pony-tailed fellow who drove from Monmouth to Chepstow — or do Stagecoach clone them? — I really do manage this time to catch the Teme Valley 802. I have a lengthy conversation with the driver but I cannot count this as in Paul Theroux style as I have been acquainted with him for some years and we merely discuss local bus topics.

In the evening, after reflecting that somewhere I must twice have crossed Julia's homeward route from West Wales as indicated by those wonderful coach names — Monmouth, perhaps, or Chepstow, but why didn't she mention Gloucester? — I settle down to study two collections of historic photographs.

One is Peter Davey's recently-published book *Bristol Tramways*.

The other is my own album of prints of Julia Dewdeney. I never surrendered the negatives. And I kept the volume of prints too…

110

Top:
The stylish Dominique — that's the coach on the left — has just gathered up the last French schoolgirls, so the girl on the right must be an inhabitant of Bath.

Above centre:
Some alleviation of the bleakness of Gloucester bus station is afforded by the frequent passage of colourful independents, the example here being Swanbrook's second- or third-hand Leyland National.

Above:
And back again to Hereford, with Stagecoach Red & White ex-West Midlands ancient hero WDA 2T to the fore, and another example of the Hereford habit of parking on double yellow lines. Rhondda, grandad and grandsons — as described in the text — set off across the road to resolve the future habitat of Rhondda's horses.

BUCKS
BUSES

KEVIN LANE looks at buses in
Buckinghamshire, past and present.

Left:

In 1975 NBC dominated the county, with United Counties buses running
in leaf green. A 1957 Bristol Lodekka operates a local service in
Bletchley. It would be withdrawn in 1976.
ALL PHOTOGRAPHS BY THE AUTHOR

Below:

Half-cab double-deckers were fast disappearing by 1980, although even
at that late date two operators were running half-cabs in Slough. London
Country still had a few Routemasters, while Alder Valley, as seen here on
a cold January day, was running FLF-series Lodekkas. An Alder Valley
Bristol RE follows.

Right:
Buckingham bus stand in 1982 with a Bedford VAM from the locally based Paynes fleet and a City of Oxford Bristol VRT loading for the trip back to Oxford. The Bedford has Plaxton's Panorama Elite body.

Below:
By the spring of 1986 Luton & District had taken over part of what had been United Counties territory and was operating this Duple-bodied Leopard coach on the Aylesbury to Heath & Reach service. It carries the short-lived Crusader Travel fleetname.

Opposite:
Buffalo Bus operated a number of local bus routes in the late 1980s and early 1990s. An ex-London Country RP-class AEC Reliance/Park Royal is seen in Bletchley in 1987.

Opposite above:
Red Rover had a long history of local bus operation and was based in Aylesbury. Here an ex-London Transport Fleetline passes through a deserted Milton Keynes centre on a Sunday in 1987. Red Rover was taken over by Luton & District at the end of that year.

Opposite below:
An ex-Ribble Atlantean in The Shires fleet — as Luton & District became in 1995 — in the green and grey livery whose history could be traced back to London Country North West, another Luton & District acquisition. It is seen in Penn, near High Wycombe, which is now served by Wycombe Bus.

Above left:
A Bristol RE belonging to Motts Travel of Aylesbury leaves the bus station at Grange School in 1988. The bus was new to United Counties and carries its original owner's fleet number in the route number box, as well as retaining its fleet number plate below the windscreen. Motts bus operations were taken over by Luton & District.

Bottom left:
Although looking like a standard NBC VRT, this bus in the Wycombe Bus fleet was in fact new to Mayne of Manchester. It is seen at Stoke Mandeville on its way from High Wycombe to Aylesbury, a route now covered by The Shires.

BUCKS
BUSES

Right:
Red Rose buses have become quite a common sight in Buckinghamshire. A 1996 Dennis Dart with UVG body leaves Aylesbury for The Claydons.

Bottom right:
Changes took place in the ownership of the main bus operator in Milton Keynes during 1997. Services are now run by MK Metro, whose fleet includes a number of Dennis Darts. This example has Carlyle bodywork.

Below:
A Leyland Olympian from The Shires fleet squeezes across the bridge between Granborough and Winslow in the autumn of 1997. It is running between Aylesbury and Buckingham.

INTERLUDE

ALISTAIR DOUGLAS abandons the dreary British winter for the warmer climes of India — and even manages a ride on a Bombay Titan.

After thoroughly enjoying a package holiday in Sri Lanka we fancied seeing something of India, but on a more independent basis. When our daughter volunteered for a spell as a medical adviser with a development agency in the South Indian state of Karnataka we decided this would be an ideal time to realise our dream. And so, in late January 1995, we found ourselves in Bombay's Sahar airport, unlike one of our bags which had gone instead to Heathrow. The KLM representative was very sympathetic and fixed us up with emergency travel kits, but the hassles we had with Customs before we finally retrieved the missing bag a couple of days later were an interesting introduction to the dreaded Indian bureaucracy.

Fortunately we had already planned to spend a couple of nights in Bombay. Immediately we experienced again the atmosphere which had so impressed us in Sri Lanka. Despite the all-too-evident grinding poverty there is a vitality all around which puts the more affluent West to shame.

It would be nice to say that we explored the city using the local buses but the thought of finding our way around on them was just too daunting. I bought a little booklet from a street vendor which listed all the BEST services as well as railway timetables, but the buses themselves displayed destinations and route numbers only in Hindu script and the conductors' command of English seemed to be similar to mine of Hindi.

Apart from one short ride to sample the famous Titan-derived half-cab deckers (when we did indeed manage to convey to the conductor our intended destination and he proved very solicitous in ensuring we alighted at the correct spot) we got around by taxi. Taxis are of course much cheaper than at home. The drivers did not appear to know their way around very well but were not reluctant to ask passers-by for directions.

There were plenty of the double-deckers around, but unfortunately none with exposed radiators nor any of the peculiarly Indian articulated models. A taxi took us to the rather small and congested bus station used by the interstate services where I saw some of the rugged vehicles employed on very long services. This is an area

Previous page:
Many of Bombay's double-deckers are in all-over advertising liveries including this one promoting the operator. The lettering on the lower side panels reads: 'Do not touch left out items. Do not leave any baggage behind.' The bus is, of course, an Ashok Leyland Titan.
ALL PHOTOGRAPHS ARE BY THE AUTHOR

Right:
A battle-scarred Ashok Leyland in central Bangalore. Note the generous ground clearance. Neither entrance nor exit has doors.

Below:
Bangalore's Central bus station has a separate section for long-distance services, which seems just a shade less chaotic than the local service departure area. All of the buses are locally-manufactured Tatas and Ashok Leylands.

adjacent to the Central railway station with pavement dwellers in the streets all around. Most state — as opposed to interstate — buses apparently terminate on a site about one hour's drive from the centre.

We flew on to Bangalore, the capital of Karnataka and said to be the fastest growing city in Asia. It is home to a rapidly developing electronics industry and is much more westernised than other Indian cities. One curiosity we found was a London Underground theme pub. However, the bus fleet is anything but modern.

The city services are operated by BTS (Bangalore Transport Services). A telephone directory in our hotel room gave a potted history. It had started as Bangalore Transport Company Ltd in 1940 with a fleet of 20 buses and had been nationalised in 1962 as BTS. A commercial road guide listed all the services, and although the destinations displayed on the buses were in the local Kannada script the route numbers were not. However, the buses were invariably so grossly overcrowded that we utilised the little auto-rickshaws. The main problem with them is that one spends so much time close to the exhausts of the ramshackle buses and, of course, the two-stroke engines of the 'autos' themselves add to the air pollution which is a feature of the Bangalore streets.

Typically, Indian front-engined single-deckers with very high floors (no DiPTAC here!) make up the bulk of the BTS fleet, but there are also a fair number of articulated and at least two front-engined double-deckers; the latter with full fronts, plus a rear-engined single-decker with a lower floor than the rest. The single-deckers all have dual entrances with the front door reserved for women and children. I was reminded of the Glasgow trams as I watched the double-deckers pull away from stops with a crowd of would-be passengers running behind trying to grab a toe- or hand-hold.

The Central bus station, adjacent to the Central railway station, is actually two huge bus stations one for BTS services and the other for longer-distance services operated by KSRTC (Karnataka State Road Transport Corporation), the bus corporations of adjoining states and

Below:
Ashok Leyland developed a rear-engined low-floor bus in the early 1980s, but did not pursue the concept with any great vigour. One of the comparatively few vehicles built is seen in Bangalore.

many private operators. The KSRTC buses, like those of BTS, are in a red livery but with white relief where the city buses are silver. The KSRTC buses usually have roof racks and do not display route numbers but, I still found it difficult to distinguish between them.

In Sri Lanka in 1993 the breakup of the Ceylon Transport Board into 'peoplised' units was well apace and competition was fierce with private buses and minibuses running on most routes. The private operators I saw in India appeared to be confined to the long-distance services, often using 'video' coaches in which, in exchange for a somewhat better standard of vehicle than that used by the state corporations, the passenger is subjected to very loud music day and night. The length and frequency of the interstate services is remarkable. For example there are 21 departures per day on a 9hr service to Madras and four on a 24hr journey to Bombay. Some city services were operated by somewhat smarter-looking buses in a fawn

Above:
Articulated semi-trailer double-deckers are a peculiarly Indian phenomenon. The billboards in the background include one promoting women's rights: 'Women are people too', it reads.

Opposite above:
Only two conventional 'deckers were encountered in Bangalore. Both were Ashok Leylands with fully-fronted bodywork.

Opposite below:
Looking decidedly modern in Bangalore Central bus station is this Hi-Tech Video Coach from Tamil Nadu.

and grey livery. I think these were owned by BTS but I could be wrong.

Soon it was time to move on to see where Margaret was working. She had booked us on the overnight Udyan Express to Raichur but, determined we should not travel like pampered Europeans, had made sure our reservations were for the ordinary three-tier sleeper. Indian rail travel is an unforgettable experience but beyond the scope of this article. Arriving very early in the morning, we would have experienced the pleasures (?) of local bus travel for the final 40-mile stage to the village of Jalahalli, but one of her colleagues gave us a lift in a Land Rover instead.

We spent two fascinating days here, sleeping on stone beds in the mud-brick guest accommodation on the campus of the development agency, SAMUHA. As well as seeing the work of the project I was interested in the rural bus services which stopped in the dusty village square. The KSRTC buses were similar to those seen in Bangalore but here I saw for the first time passengers, sometimes very many passengers, travelling on the roof racks. This is a common, albeit illegal, practice away from the larger cities. The buses already have a high centre of gravity, even without passengers or heavy luggage on the roof, and are prone to roll over after even minor collisions. Several cases were reported in the newspapers during our stay and we passed one bus on its side in Hampi.

SAMUHA, among other things, promotes women's development and one item in its newsletter is worth recounting here. A village had lost its bus service due to the poor state of the road but the service had not been resumed after the road was repaired. The women decided to take action:

Right:
Rickshaws await custom at Hospet bus station as a Karnataka State RTC Tata pulls away. Some considerable agility is needed to reach the roof-rack, using the rear wheel as a starting point for the climb up to the exceedingly short ladder.

Opposite:
An Ashok Leyland Viking of the Karnataka State RTC negotiates the throng in Hospet main street.

Below:
An Ashok Leyland in the Karnataka State Road Transport Corporation fleet. The roof-mounted luggage rack carries a spare wheel. Ashok Leyland is now associated with the Italian-based Iveco group.

'We went in a group to the depot manager in Deodurg on a bullock cart. We didn't know where to go. But we found our way to the depot by asking people on the way. At the depot, the officials were surprised to seeing [sic] a group of women come to demand something from them. It was probably the first time they were faced with something like this. We talked to the manager, placed our demand and he promised to do the needful within two weeks. To our surprise we got the bus even earlier than that.'

The ruined city of Vijayanagar (Hampi) is a historical site to rival Pompeii or the Pyramids but, I am ashamed to say, I had never heard of it. It is less than 100 miles from Jalahalli and some of Margaret's Indian colleagues arranged the hire of a Land Rover to take us there. Seven in a Land Rover is a bit of a crush but nothing compared to the buses. After showing us some of the wonders of this once wealthy city destroyed in the 16th century they had to return, but we spent the night in the small town of Hospet so that we could see more of Hampi before making another overnight train journey back to Bangalore.

I was, of course, attracted to the busy bus station in Hospet and thought we might use the frequent KSRTC service to Hampi. An auto-rickshaw driver who had already offered to take us for a ridiculously small fare waited patiently as we watched the scramble to board and cling to the bus, smiled knowingly and repeated his offer. For the less agile, or lazier passengers, it is apparently common practice to hand a bag through a window to an alighting friend so that he can reserve a seat.

At Hampi there were a great many coaches from all parts of India which had brought pilgrims to this holy site. They were obviously cooking and sleeping in, around or under the coaches for the duration of their stay and the area was a hive of activity.

After a few more days in Bangalore it was time to return home, again flying via Bombay. The BEST buses which had seemed rather battered only a couple of weeks ago now looked in pristine condition by comparison with those we had left behind in Karnataka.

One thing most people probably associate with India is the dreaded Delhi belly. We have suffered stomach upsets in many places much nearer home but had no problems throughout this holiday. I think this has much to do with the fact that we never used any of the large tourist hotels, eating mainly in small local establishments where the food was cooked to order. It was economical too. In Lingsugur, on the way to Hampi, seven of us enjoyed an excellent breakfast for less than the price of a single hamburger at home.

Below:

Pilgrims and their transport — a Tata — at Hampi. The roof-rack is well laden. Many rural roads are unmade which may explain the missing nearside windscreen. It also explains why most Indian buses and coaches have flat glass windscreens, as on the vehicle in the background.

GLASGOW'S
MILES BETTER

Scotland's biggest city suffered rapid decline as its traditional heavy industries disappeared in the 1960s. But during the 1970s and 1980s it underwent a remarkable renaissance, justifying its claim 'Glasgow's miles better'. Glasgow resident BILLY NICOL illustrates the Strathclyde Buses fleet in the days before FirstBus.

Right:
The low-height version of the Alexander R-type has shallower side windows — compare the relationship of the upper deck windscreen with the side windows on this Olympian with the Citybus illustrated below. Strathclyde Buses received 52 Olympians in 1993, the last Leyland-built models for UK service.
ALL PHOTOGRAPHS BY THE AUTHOR

Below:
This Alexander-bodied Volvo Citybus carries the advertising which underlined Glasgow's new-found confidence. Strathclyde Buses was the biggest customer for the Citybus, taking 95 in 1989-90.

Right:
A fire at Strathclyde Buses' Larkfield garage in 1992 destroyed 60 buses. To cover this a variety of different types were hired or purchased from other operators. The hired buses included 18 Tayside Ailsas which had Strathclyde's orange livery applied to the front panels.

Below:
Full-size single-deckers play a small part in Strathclyde's operations. This Volvo B10B with Northern Counties bodywork was evaluated in 1993, but none was bought. It was later sold by Volvo to Whitelaw of Stonehouse.

Above:
While Alexander has been the main supplier of bodywork to Strathclyde Buses, it certainly hasn't been the only one. In 1995 four Volvo-built Olympians were purchased, two of which had Northern Counties Palatine II bodies. They were soon transferred to the sister Kelvin Central fleet, but 10 further Palatine IIs were purchased in 1997.

Left:
Soon after being sold to its management and employees in 1993, Strathclyde set up a low-cost unit which traded as GCT — the initials of Glasgow Corporation Transport. It used a dark green and yellow livery, not dissimilar to a scheme used by the Strathclyde PTE in the early 1980s. An Atlantean in GCT colours stands at Govan bus station.

Top right:
Strathclyde started operating to East Kilbride, and for one of the routes required low-height buses. The first were Leyland Olympians with ECW bodies. One is seen in Glasgow city centre in 1993.

Below right:
Strathclyde was a pioneer in small bus operation, running minibuses in the early 1980s long before they became fashionable. Deregulation saw the widespread use of small buses, and most of these were MCW MetroRiders including five ex-Colchester buses acquired in 1991. This MetroRider is seen in central Paisley.

Bottom right:
Coaches played a small part in the Strathclyde business and included some odd vehicles, such as this 1989 MCW Metrobus II, rebuilt with high-backed seats. Metrobus coaches were used for local private hires and for excursions — which sometimes took them as far south as Blackpool. This one is seen in Glasgow's Argyle Street, heading no further south than East Kilbride.